CELTIC CROSS STITCH

30 alphabet, animal and knotwork projects

GAIL LAWTHER

David & Charles

Photography by Di Lewis

Book design by Christopher Lawther

Printed in Italy by New Interlitho SpA

for David & Charles
Brunel House   Newton Abbot   Devon

CELTIC
CROSS STITCH

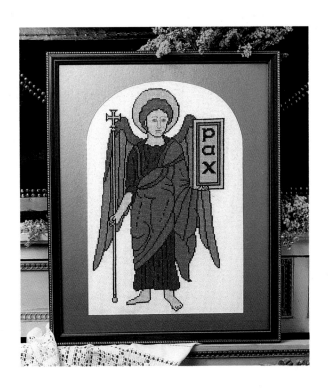

CONTENTS

Introduction   7

KNOTS AND PATTERNS   13
Cross Bookmark   14
Trinket Box   16
Knotwork Greetings Cards   18
Decorated Hand-towel   20
Dolls' House Rug   22
Table-mats and Napkins   24
Celtic Jewellery   26
Knotwork Picture   28
Embroidered Christening Robe   30
Square Cushion   32

ANIMALS AND PEOPLE   37
Horse Card and Picture   38
Baby's Bib   40
Peacock Waistcoat   42
Lion Picture   46
Serpent Pincushion   48
Stained-glass Angel   51
Cockerel Sweatshirt   54
Curtain Tie-back   56
Horseman Picture   60
Celtic Rug   64

LETTERING   69
Initial Cards   70
Stitched Nameplate   78
Pincushion and Needlecase   80
Bright Sampler   86
Noel Christmas Decoration   90
Wedding Initials   92
Initial Pictures   100
Tie and Handkerchief   107
Versal Sampler   109
Illuminated Initial   112

PATTERN LIBRARY   115
Knots   115
Knotwork Borders   118
Fret and Key Patterns   120
Animals   122
Letterforms   124

Acknowledgements   127
Bibliography   127
Index   128

INTRODUCTION

When we see a particular kind of interweaving knotwork pattern we immediately recognise it as a Celtic design: but who were the Celts and why has their art been so influential? 'Celtic' usually describes the peoples of Western Europe, the groups who spoke – or speak – languages similar to those of the ancient Gauls: Breton, Cornish, Welsh, Irish, Manx and Gaelic. Several Scandinavian countries are also rich sources of Celtic art.

The Celtic period of history is even harder to define, partly because it occurred in different countries or regions at different times. The roots of Celtic art and patterns lie in traditional Anglo-Saxon designs: the jewellery found at Sutton Hoo dates from pre-Christian times, but shows knotwork animal patterns similar to the ones associated with later Celtic art. The style found its real flowering, though, in religious books, carvings and artefacts as Christianity swept across pagan Western Europe. Celtic art began in Ireland in the fifth and sixth centuries, and continued until at least the ninth century, providing us with a wonderful visual record of the period at the end of the Dark Ages.

MOTIFS IN CELTIC ART

The motifs of Celtic art are many and varied. The wonderful interweaving knots are famous, of course, and were especially popular with Celtic artists, but many other patterns were also worked: key and fret designs were frequently used and their borders and panels were often elaborate mixtures of squares, circles and rectangles. As well as these, animal and bird forms, both realistic and fantastic, occur frequently, while humans and angels were

Horse card and picture, see page 38

very often the subjects of illuminations.

The letters themselves are rich inspirations for modern artists. The letterforms range from relatively simple uncial and half-uncial forms – used for the body of text in books – through to the opulence of the richly illuminated initial letters – sometimes so large that they almost fill an entire page.

In the projects for this book I have taken inspiration from all these different sources, building them into a wide variety of items ranging from samplers and monograms to pincushions, rugs, cards and pictures. Like Celtic art itself, some of my designs are realistic, while others are highly stylised.

COLOURS

There is no such thing as a typical Celtic colour-scheme; Celtic artists had an instinctive colour sense which included unlikely combinations as well as those we would consider harmonious. A flip through a book of facsimiles of Celtic illuminations takes you from subtle pastels placed side by side, through rich dark combinations of red, brown and ochre, to lurid yellow/green/red/black mixtures and rainbow combinations of purple/green/red/yellow/jade/ pink/orange and blue. Sometimes the colours used are pure and bright; at other times they are toned down by the addition of grey or brown, or diluted to pastels with white or beige.

To represent these varied styles in Celtic art, I have chosen many different colour-schemes. For example, the cards on page 70 use bright colour-schemes taken direct from their inspiration, the *Book of Kells*; and the horseman on page 60 uses a wide range of impure colours, matching the realistic style of the figure and the horse.

ADAPTING THE DESIGNS FOR CROSS STITCH

The flowing lines of most Celtic designs are quite a challenge for the cross stitch designer, as they have to flow realistically while being worked on a regular grid! This is especially difficult for some of the letters, as they rely on carefully weighted and angled lines for their attractiveness. The great benefit, though, is that some of the designs, especially the regular knots, such as the dolls' house rug on page 22, can be worked out first on a simple formula, and then can be adapted easily to fit a larger, smaller or differently proportioned rectangle.

If you want to try to work out your own Celtic designs or vary the ones in the book, begin with a simple knot and make a few adaptations. The example below, for instance, is very straightforward, but lends itself to all kinds of variations once you have worked out the correct relationship of the interweaving lines. Make sure that you keep this relationship constant, then you can play around with the shape, size and number of strands almost *ad infinitum*, just on one simple knot design!

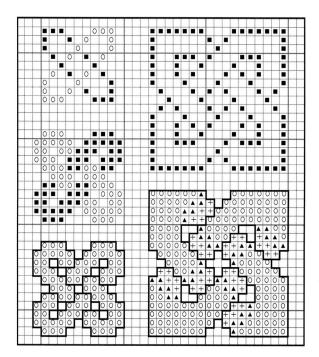

CROSS-STITCH TIPS

If you are an experienced cross stitcher, you will already have all the skills needed to tackle the projects in this book. If you are a beginner, you will find some of the larger projects more challenging than the smaller, simpler ones, but they should all be within your scope if you follow a few basic guidelines.

Some people prefer to work both parts of each stitch – the bottom diagonal stitch and then the top one – before they move onto the next stitch.

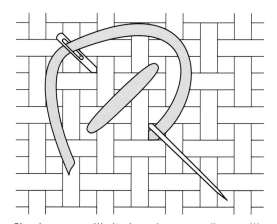

Single cross stitch showing needle position

Others prefer to stitch a row or a column of half-stitches before working their way back along the row and crossing with the top stitches. Either of these ways is satisfactory; there is no 'correct' way to stitch – it depends on which method you prefer. If you are a beginner, experiment with both techniques and see which gives you the most even tension; the stitches should lie flat so that the threads are not distorted and they should not pull the fabric out of shape.

The main thing to remember is that the top stitch of each cross should always be in the same direction so that the finished work has an even texture and the stitches all catch the light the same way. While you are stitching, especially if you are working on a large project

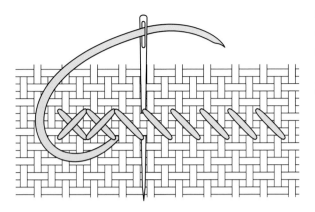

Part completed stitches – completed on return journey

with lots of repetitive movements, you may find that your thread becomes tightly twisted and keeps knotting back on itself. If this happens, simply let the needle and thread hang down loosely from the work so that it can untwist itself. If you have the opposite problem, and your thread keeps coming untwisted so that the strands separate, just make a small twist with your needle every few stitches so that the thread maintains a better texture.

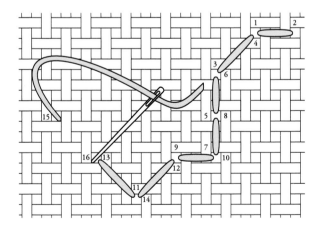

WORKING BACK STITCH OUTLINES

As well as cross stitch, you will also need back stitch for working outlines on some of the charts. Back stitch outlining is worked by

stitching single back stitches, the width or height of one cross stitch, around all or some of the sides of specified cross stitches.

MATERIALS

Cross stitch is generally worked on some kind of **even-weave** fabric; this means a fabric that has strong threads running vertically and horizontally, with obvious holes between the threads. Even-weave fabrics are usually described as being so many hpi, or holes per inch (2.5cm), and vary from fine fabrics, such as **linens** and **silk gauze**, which may be 25-30hpi, through to very coarse fabrics such as **binca**, which is often 6hpi. Because there are obvious holes in even-weave fabrics, you don't need a sharp needle – in fact, a sharp needle is a definite disadvantage because it may split the threads when you are trying to find the right hole. On these fabrics, tapestry needles are used; they come in different sizes, from very fine (sizes 26-28) to very large (sizes 16-18), and have rounded tips. Each project specifies either a fine, medium or large tapestry needle; I have not specified an exact size, as this is very much a matter of personal preference.

Other even-weave backgrounds are suitable for cross stitch. Ordinary **canvas** is satisfactory, but has the disadvantage that it is transparent, so you have to cover the whole area that will show with stitching; with even-weave fabric such as **Aida**, you only need to stitch the design – it is not necessary to cover the background. **Cross-stitch paper** is also on the market and is available in a variety of colours; it is best for small projects, such as Christmas decorations or cards, as it is not very durable and becomes worn easily if you are stitching on one piece for a long time. **Plastic canvas** is available in several gauges and colours; this is a firm plastic mesh that can be built up into 3-D shapes.

If you want to stitch a cross-stitch pattern on to a fabric that is not even-weave, such as a sweatshirt or a T-shirt, this is possible using the method known as **waste canvas**. Waste canvas looks like conventional canvas; you cut out a piece and tack it on to your chosen background fabric, then stitch the design over the threads of the canvas and through the background simultaneously. You must have a sharp-tipped needle, such as a crewel, for this technique. When the design is complete, you dampen the threads of the waste canvas, which dissolves the glue holding them together; they can then be withdrawn from behind the stitching, leaving your cross-stitch design on the background fabric.

THREADS

Cross stitch can be done in virtually any thread as long as you choose the right background, but some threads are more versatile than others. **Stranded cotton (floss)** is always a favourite, as it comes in so many shades and can be used in several different thicknesses; **coton perlé** has a pleasant sheen, and is good for projects that don't require a fine thread. **Coton à broder** is a fairly fine, single-strand cotton thread. **Marlitt** is a viscose thread that is very shiny, but also very slippery; it can be used in several different thicknesses. Many **metallic threads** are on the market; some are more successful than others for cross stitch, but if you treat them carefully it is usually possible to adapt them; they also look good mixed in with stranded cotton (floss) to provide a bit of sparkle. **Soft cotton, tapestry yarn, knitting yarns** and other thick threads can also be used successfully for cross stitch on larger-gauge backgrounds.

Each of the projects is accompanied by a chart on which you will find a colour key for the threads used. It is assumed that you will buy one skein of each colour mentioned (although less may be used), unless the key specifies two or more skeins. Each chart key gives both Anchor and DMC colours; generally these can be intermingled, unless the project specifies otherwise.

EXTRA EQUIPMENT

As well as needles, threads and fabrics, you will also need the usual extra equipment that you probably have in your sewing-box: a thimble if you like using one; small, sharp scissors; a tape measure; larger scissors for trimming.

MARKING METHODS

One very useful piece of equipment is a water-soluble pen; this pen makes turquoise marks on the background fabric, but the marks disappear when they are wetted, which makes it ideal for marking positions on your fabrics before stitching. When you dampen the fabric to make the marks disappear, don't iron it until the fabric is completely dry, otherwise you may get brown blotches where the pen marks have been. Fading pens are also available, which make purple marks that disappear in daylight, but as the marks only last about 24 hours, this can be frustrating if you need a mark on the fabric for longer! Lines of tacking to mark the centre-point can also be used if you prefer.

FRAMES

If you like using a frame, or find that your tension tends to pull a little too tightly without one, by all means use a frame for your work, but there is generally no need to; the background fabric rarely pulls out of true if you keep the tension of your stitches even. If the fabric is not quite square when you have finished the design, simply dampen the fabric, pull it into shape, then iron on the back with a steam iron.

PRESSING CROSS STITCH

When pressing your completed cross stitch, or any other embroidery, lay the design face down

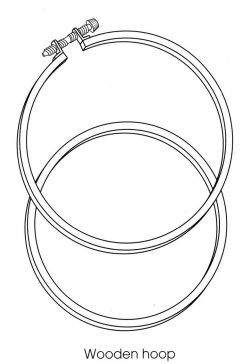

Wooden hoop

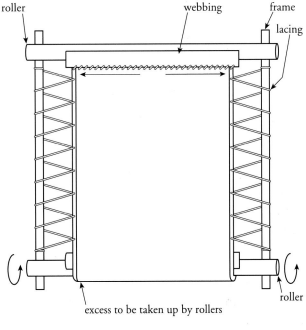

Rotating frame

on a soft surface such as a pale towel, and iron from the back; this prevents the stitching from being squashed. If you have used a water-soluble pen on a project, it is safe to iron on a steam setting as long as you have let the fabric dry out completely first time round after sponging out the marks.

USING THE CHARTS

Each square on each chart represents one cross stitch worked in the colour specified on the key for that particular square. A thick line around part of a square represents one back stitch, also worked in the colour specified on the key. So, the chart shown below results in the piece of

stitching which is shown next to it.

Each project carries a design size and stitch count at the beginning. The design size describes the dimensions of the finished design when it is stitched on the specified fabric. The stitch count gives the number of stitches across the width and height of the design.

If you want to adapt the design to a smaller or larger gauge of fabric, the stitch count will enable you to work out exactly how much fabric you need. Do remember, though, that you may need to adjust the thickness and amount of the threads needed if you are working the design on either a larger or smaller scale.

KEY			
DMC 961	Anchor 76	+	Dark pink
DMC 3716	Anchor 75	▲	Mid-pink
DMC 818	Anchor 48	O	Light pink
DMC 550	Anchor 102	–	Purple

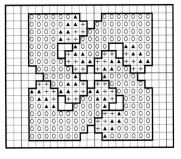

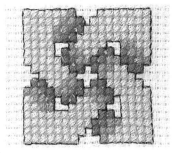

KNOTS AND PATTERNS

The ten projects in this section all feature patterns based on Celtic designs. Knotwork designs are what many people think of first when they picture Celtic art; lines of jewel-bright colours or softer pastels continuously intertwining. Knots in Celtic art vary from simple twists, through more complex plaits and borders, to the elaborate carpet pages – whole pages in illuminated manuscripts dedicated to labyrinthine interweavings.

The Celts believed that the lines of knotwork showed the twist, flow and complexity of life, and that the single-line knot echoed eternity. Their artists made knotwork designs fit into any available space; the benefit of the undulating lines is that they can be made to meander in any direction! From only one or two separate lines, elaborate borders can be built up and made to go around corners or fit into cross shapes or T-shapes.

The knotwork patterns in the following projects follow that tradition, and feature circles, rectangles, squares, diamonds, triangles, borders and quarter-circles in both simple and complex patterns.

Spirals, too, were popular with the Celts – they liked movement and flow in their patterns. They also favoured key and fret patterns, ornamental designs similar to Greek patterns or upright zigzags that generally fit into squares; the squares can then be joined in repeat patterns or borders, or fitted into stepped pyramids. Spirals and fret patterns are featured in the jewellery designs on page 26, and also appear on pages 120-121 in the pattern library.

CROSS BOOKMARK

C|eltic cross designs range from the simple to the elaborate – sometimes built up from knots or spirals, sometimes incorporating animals or birds. This design was based on a cross cut in marble in the old cathedral at Chur, Switzerland; although the knot looks complex, it is actually a fairly simple repeat.

Stitch count: 71 x 131
Design size: 6 x 6in (15 x 7.5cm)

MATERIALS

- One piece of white Aida or other even-weave fabric, 22hpi, 10 x 6in (25 x 15cm)
- Stranded cotton (floss): green
- Fine tapestry needle

PRODUCING THE DESIGN

1 Press the fabric and fold it in half down the length to find the centre line; mark this with a water-soluble pen.

2 Measure 1¹/2in (4cm) from the top of the fabric down the marked line and mark this point with the water-soluble pen; this is where you will begin your stitching.

3 Using only one strand of cotton (floss) in the needle, work three cross stitches side by side, so that the middle one falls on the centre line at your marked point. These three stitches are the ones at the centre top of the charted design.

4 Continue working the stitches following the chart, using one strand of cotton (floss) throughout. Keep checking that the lines of stitches match across the central line, so that you will know if you have miscounted at any stage.

5 When the embroidery is complete, sponge away the water-soluble pen marks. Press the embroidery on the back (see page 10).

6 Using sharp scissors, cut any excess fabric away from the top and sides of the embroidery to within six threads of the stitching. Cut the bottom 1¹/2in (4cm) down from the stitching. Fray three double threads away from each edge of the bookmark, and press again on the reverse.

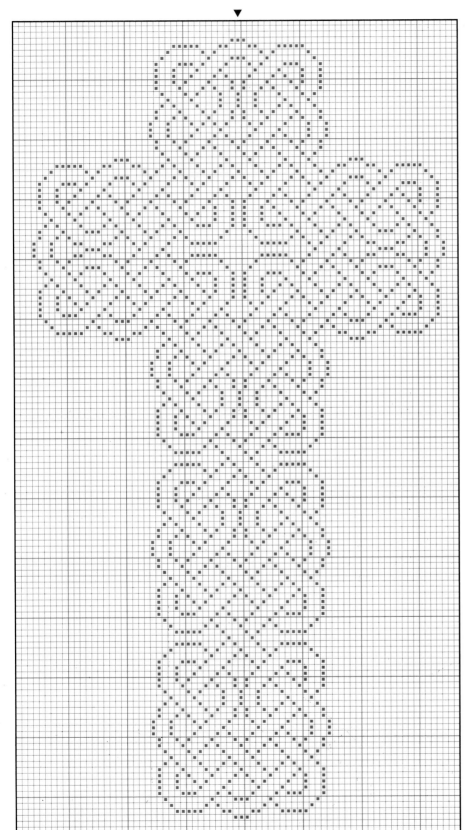

VARIATION

If you prefer a simpler cross design, you could try the more straightforward one on page 116 of the pattern library, filling in the central parts with a paler colour.

KEY
DMC 699
Anchor 923 ■ Green

TRINKET BOX

This pretty circular design can be used on a square or circular trinket-box base; stitch it in the colourway shown here, or choose your own colours to fit in with your bedroom.

Stitch count: 57 x 57
Design size: $4^1/4$ x $4^1/4$in (11 x 11cm)

MATERIALS
For a box with a $4^3/4$-$5^1/2$in (12-14cm) square or circular aperture, you will need:
- One piece of pale turquoise damask Aida, 14hpi, 8 x 8in (20 x 20cm)
- Stranded cottons (floss) in the colours given in the key
- Medium tapestry needle

PRODUCING THE DESIGN

1 Fold the square of fabric in half lengthways and press the fold gently, then fold it in half widthways and press again. Where the folds cross marks the centre of the fabric square.

2 Using two strands of purple and beginning at the centre of the design, follow the dark squares on the chart to work all of the purple outline stitches of the knot.

3 Use the purple to stitch the small patterns at the corners of the design.

4 Using two strands of turquoise cotton, fill in the inside parts of the knot; because you have worked all the outlines you should not need to count the squares.

5 Lay the completed embroidery face down on a soft surface and press it from the back (see page 10).

6 Depending on the box that you are using, the exact way of inserting the embroidery into it will differ; the box you buy should come with instructions. Generally the process involves trimming the fabric to a given size, slipping it into a recess or over a padded section of the lid, then securing it in position with some kind of backing piece.

KEY

DMC 552	Anchor 101	■	Purple
DMC 3761	Anchor 9159	O	Turquoise

VARIATION

You can stitch this design at different sizes to suit the different sizes of trinket boxes on the market.
Choose your box first, then see what hpi fabric you need in order to fit the design into the aperture (see page 11).

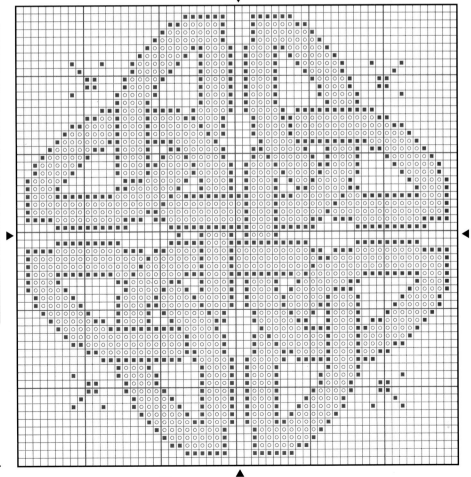

KNOTWORK GREETINGS CARDS

Two very different knotwork designs appear on these cards. The bright heraldic design would suit any occasion; the fan shape incorporates a heart and would be particularly suitable for a wedding, anniversary or Valentine card.

Stitch count: Pink fan card 47 x 31
Multi-coloured card 57 x 57
Design size: Pink fan card 4 x 3in (10 x 7.5cm)
Multi-coloured card 4 x 4in (10 x 10cm)

MATERIALS

For the multi-coloured card you will need:

- One piece of cream Aida, 14hpi, 10 x 10in (25 x 25cm)
- Stranded cottons (floss) in the colours given in the key
- One spool of metallic thread, Madeira No 40, turquoise
- Fine tapestry needle
- Large pale jade card blank with an aperture at least 7 x 7in (18 x 18cm)

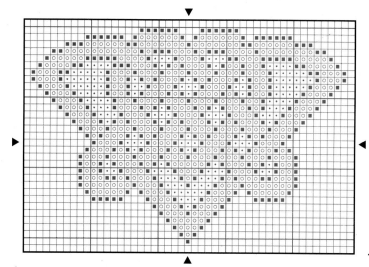

KEY			
For the multi-coloured card:			
DMC 743	Anchor 302	▨	Dark yellow
DMC 744	Anchor 301	▨	Light yellow
DMC 826	Anchor 155	▨	Blue
DMC 3814	Anchor 189	▨	Dark green
DMC 958	Anchor 187	▨	Light green
Madeira No 40		–	Turquoise
For the pink fan card:			
DMC 961	Anchor 76	■	Dark pink
DMC 3716	Anchor 75	O	Mid-pink
DMC 818	Anchor 48	•	Light pink

For the pink fan card you will need:

- One piece of cream Aida, 11hpi, 7 x 6in (18 x 15cm)
- Stranded cottons (floss) in the colours given in the key
- Medium tapestry needle
- One small piece of thin wadding (batting)
- Large pale pink card blank with a quarter-circle aperture

PRODUCING THE DESIGNS

1 For the multi-coloured card, fold the square of Aida in half diagonally, and press gently. Unfold it and press gently in the other direction; where the folds cross is the centre of the fabric and corresponds with the central square of the charted design for the multi-coloured card.

2 Using two strands of thread for all the cross stitches, stitch the design in the appropriate colours; begin at the centre of the fabric and chart and work outwards.

3 Using one strand of turquoise metallic thread, outline the edges of the design with back stitch (see page 9) as marked on the chart.

4 For the pink fan card, fold the cream Aida in half so that the sides meet, and press gently. Measure up $1^{1}/2$in (4cm) from the bottom of the fabric along the central fold, and begin your stitching at this point; it corresponds to the tip of the fan on the chart.

5 Using three strands of thread throughout, stitch the design in the appropriate colours, following the chart. When making up the card place the wadding behind the Aida.

6 Press both embroideries from the back (see page 10) then follow the instructions on page 71 for making them into cards.

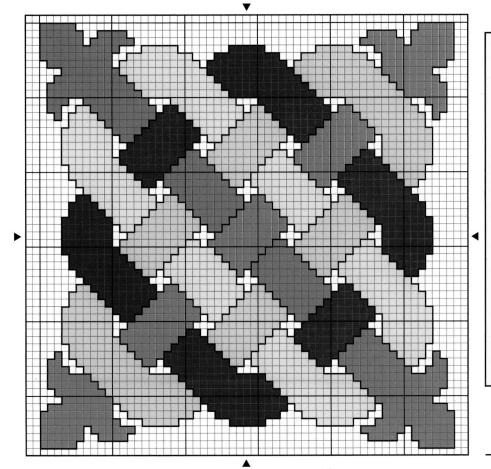

VARIATIONS

The fan design can be stitched in colours other than pink; try it in royal colours with a fine gold back stitch (see page 9) around the edges. The design is made up from one line; for an unusual effect, try shading subtly from one colour to another as you work around the knot.

DECORATED HAND-TOWEL

$\mathcal{T}$ he distinctive knotwork border designs are some of the most attractive features of Celtic art; this hand-towel makes use of a complex knot in two colours.

Stitch count: 35 deep
Design size: 2^1/$_2$in (6.5cm) deep

MATERIALS
- One maroon hand-towel with a band specially for working cross stitch. The one illustrated is Classic Manner by Crafter's Pride, colour cranberry. The stitching band should be at least 35 squares deep
- Stranded cottons (floss) in the colours given in the key
- Medium tapestry needle

PRODUCING THE DESIGN
1 Fold the stitching band of your towel in half so that the sides meet, and press. This pressed line will be the centre line of your first motif.

2 Count to find the centre of your stitching band from top to bottom. Where this line meets the pressed line will mark the exact centre of your first motif.

3 Using three strands of stranded cotton (floss) for all the cross stitches, follow the chart to stitch the pink and blue portions of one whole motif.

4 Stitch as many whole repeats of the motif as you can fit in to each side of the central one; each complete repeat takes twenty-four stitches widthways.

5 Finish off the pink and blue lines of stitching with the decorative finials shown on the chart; each finial requires nine stitches widthways, so make sure that you have space after your final motifs.

6 Using two strands of maroon cotton, work back stitches (see page 9) over each of the lines marked on the chart – the places where the knotwork lines cross themselves or each other.

7 When all the stitching is complete, press the embroidery from the back (see page 10).

VARIATIONS

Try using one of the other border patterns from the pattern library on pages 118-119 to decorate your towels; work a narrow one on the smaller towels and a more complex one on wider Aida tape for bath sheets.

If you do not want to use a towel with a section woven in for cross stitch, you can buy one of the specially made Aida bands and work your design onto that. The bands come in several different colours, widths and styles.

If you prefer, work both of the knotwork lines in the same colour and just show where they overlap with the back stitches.

KEY

DMC 813	Anchor 977	●	Light blue
DMC 604	Anchor 60	+	Pink
DMC 3803	Anchor 43	–	Maroon

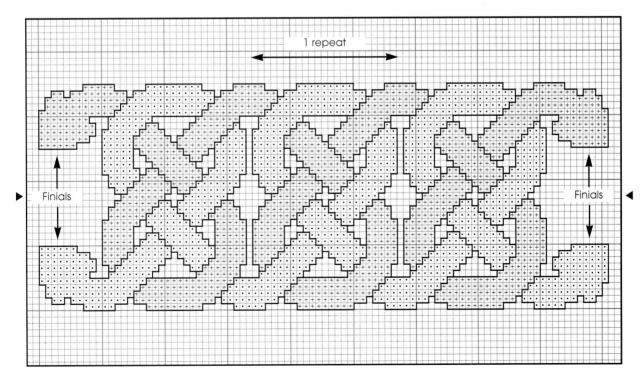

1 repeat

Finials

Finials

DOLLS' HOUSE RUG

Celtic designs can be used to decorate not only your own house: this miniature rug will be just the right size for a dolls' house. The tiny cross stitches, similar to *petit point*, produce a firm, hard-wearing texture, and the ends of the fabric are frayed out to make the fringes of the rug.

> **Stitch count:** 61 x 45
> **Design size:** $3^1/4$ x $2^1/4$in(8.5 x 6cm)

MATERIALS

- One piece of cream Aida, 22hpi, 6 x $4^3/4$in (15 x 12cm)
- One piece of iron-on stiffening fabric, $3^1/2$ x $2^1/2$in (8.5 x 6cm)
- Stranded cottons (floss) in the colours given in the key
- Fine tapestry needle

PRODUCING THE DESIGN

1. Fold the Aida in half lengthwise and press lightly to mark the fold, then fold it in half widthways and press. Mark these lines with a water-soluble pen; they will be the centre lines of your design.
2. Using one strand of dark blue, work the stitches outlining the knot, beginning at the centre of the chart and fabric and working outwards.
3. Using one strand of light blue, fill in all the areas inside the knot outlines.
4. Using one strand of cream, fill in all the

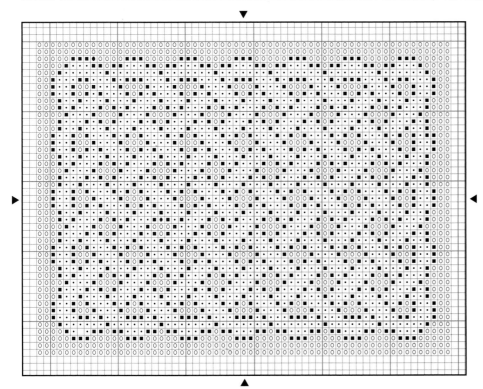

background areas within the pattern and outside it as marked on the chart.

5 When the embroidery is complete, spray or sponge the fabric to remove the pen marks. Allow it to dry completely. Trim the fabric to $^1/_2$in (1cm) beyond the stitching all around the edges of the design. Fray the top and bottom edges of the rectangle up to the stitching.

6 Lay the embroidery face down and fold the spare fabric around the sides to the back of the embroidery. Position the rectangle of iron-on stiffening fabric, adhesive side down, over the back of the embroidery, and fuse it into place with a hot iron.

PRACTICAL TIP

When you are ironing the stiffening fabric onto the back of the rug, simply lay the hot iron on top of the fabric and press down; if you use the usual to-and-fro ironing motion, the fabric may ruck up.

KEY

DMC 809	Anchor 175	•	Light blue
DMC 797	Anchor 177	■	Dark blue
DMC Ecru	Anchor 885	0	Cream

VARIATIONS

If blue and cream do not match the décor of your dolls' house, pick out colours from your carpet or curtains and work the chart in those. Use a darker and lighter version of the same colour for the knot itself, or combine two different ones, such as blue and peach, green and beige, orange and pale green.

To change the feel of the rug radically, work the knot in pale and medium shades of one colour, and work the background in a darker colour such as charcoal, navy or burgundy; this would look particularly effective if you have a period dolls' house.

TABLE-MATS AND NAPKINS

A cornerpiece from a richly illuminated letter 'B' was the inspiration for this right-angled knot. The design is worked on an even-weave fabric with 28 threads to the inch (2.5cm), but it can just as easily be worked on a piece of Aida or binca at different sizes.

Stitch count: 49 x 49
Design size: 5½ x 5½in (14 x 14cm)

MATERIALS

For a set comprising one mat and one table-napkin you will need:

- Two pieces of pale green even-weave fabric, 28hpi; one rectangle measuring 20 x 15in (50 x 38cm), and one square measuring 15 x 15in (38 x 38cm)
- Matching sewing thread
- Coton à broder in the colours given in the key
- Medium tapestry needle

PRODUCING THE DESIGN

1 Turn under and press a small double hem around each piece of fabric, then sew by hand or machine. It is best to do this before you start the embroidery, partly to stop the fabric from fraying and partly so that you can make sure that you position the design evenly on each piece. Press the hemmed pieces before stitching.

2 Measure 2¾in (7cm) diagonally in from the top right and bottom left corners of the

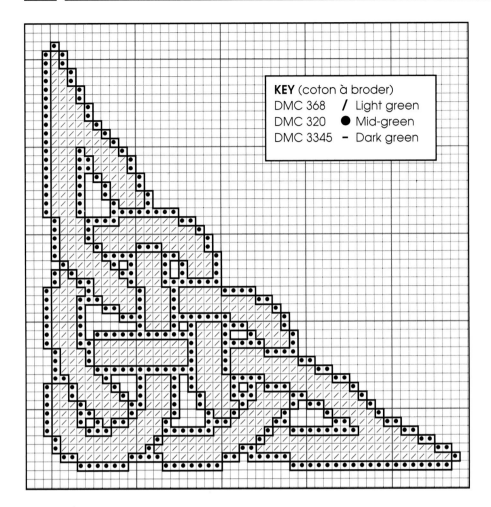

KEY (coton à broder)
DMC 368   **/** Light green
DMC 320   **●** Mid-green
DMC 3345 **–** Dark green

table-mat, and from one corner of the napkin. Mark the place with a dot of water-soluble pen, and use these marks as guides for the corners of your designs.

3 Using one strand of coton à broder across three threads of the background fabric, stitch the outline crosses of the design in mid-green. Fill in the areas marked inside the knot design with crosses in pale green.

4 Using one strand of dark green, work around the outside edges of the outline stitches in back stitch (see page 9). Make each back stitch across the width of one cross stitch — that is, across three threads of background fabric each time.

5 Once the designs are complete, remove the dots from the water-soluble pen with a dab of

water. Let the fabric dry completely, then lay the mat and napkin face down on a soft cloth and press the designs on the back with a steam iron (see page 10).

PRACTICAL TIP

If the fabric of your table linen is not even-weave, use waste canvas (see page 10) as a stitching guide for your cornerpieces.

VARIATIONS

As the knot fits so well into a right angle, use the design for the corner of a bag, a curtain or a cushion as well as for all kinds of table linen.

CELTIC JEWELLERY

Rich colours and the addition of gold threads give these simple jewellery designs the opulence of gilded illuminations. The pendant is stitched straight onto a pre-punched metal blank, manufactured especially for cross stitch; the brooch is stitched on a fine even-weave fabric.

Stitch count: for the brooch 21 x 29
Design size: for the brooch 1³/₄ x 1¹/₄in (4.5 x 3cm)

MATERIALS

For the pendant you will need:
- One Gold'n Cross Stitch gold-plated pendant blank
- Stranded cottons (floss) in the colours given in the key
- One spool of gold embroidery thread such as Madeira No 40, gold 7
- Medium tapestry needle

For the brooch you will need:
- One gilt oval brooch blank, approximately 1¹/₂ x 2in (4 x 5cm)
- One piece of white Aida, 18hpi, approximately 4in (10cm) square

- Stranded cotton (floss) in the colour given in the key
- One spool of gold embroidery thread such as Madeira No 40, gold 7
- Fine tapestry needle

PRODUCING THE DESIGNS

To make the pendant:
1 Using three strands of cotton (floss), follow the chart to stitch the design on the metal blank in blue and jade.
2 Using two strands of gold thread, work back stitch (see page 9) around the edges of the knot as shown on the chart.

To make the brooch:
1 Fold the square of Aida in half diagonally and press gently; fold diagonally in the other direction and press. Where the folds meet is the centre of the fabric.
2 Beginning at the centre of the fabric and the centre of the chart, stitch the spiral design in one strand of red.
3 Using one strand of gold thread, work back stitch (see page 9) around the edges of the design as shown on the chart.
4 Trim the fabric and assemble the brooch according to the manufacturer's instructions.

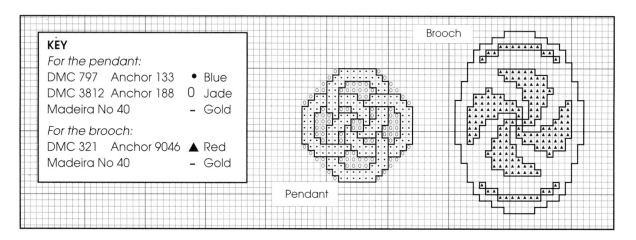

KEY
For the pendant:
DMC 797   Anchor 133   • Blue
DMC 3812   Anchor 188   0 Jade
Madeira No 40   – Gold

For the brooch:
DMC 321   Anchor 9046   ▲ Red
Madeira No 40   – Gold

Brooch

Pendant

VARIATIONS

Many other simple Celtic designs can be substituted for the two shown in the photograph; here are some alternative designs in different shapes.

RNOTWORR PICTURE

Many Celtic knotwork designs can be made into simple pictures; this circular design, based on four heart shapes and edged in gold, is surrounded by a creamy-yellow mount in a plain gold frame.

Stitch count: 49 x 49
Design size: 3 1/2 x 3 1/2in (9 x 9cm)

MATERIALS
- One piece of cream Aida, 14hpi, 6 1/4in (16cm) square
- Stranded cottons (floss) in the colours given in the key
- One spool of gold embroidery thread such as Gütermann metallic 24, or Madeira No 40, gold 7
- Medium tapestry needle
- One 5 1/2in (14cm) square picture frame, with or without mount

PRODUCING THE DESIGN
1 Fold the fabric in half lengthwise and press lightly, then fold it in half widthways and press. Where the two folds cross is the centre of your design.
2 Using two strands of cotton (floss), and beginning at the centre of the chart and the fabric and working outwards, stitch the design, following the colours as they are marked on the chart.
3 Using two strands of gold thread, work back stitches (see page 9) all round the outside edges of the knotwork line as marked on the chart opposite.

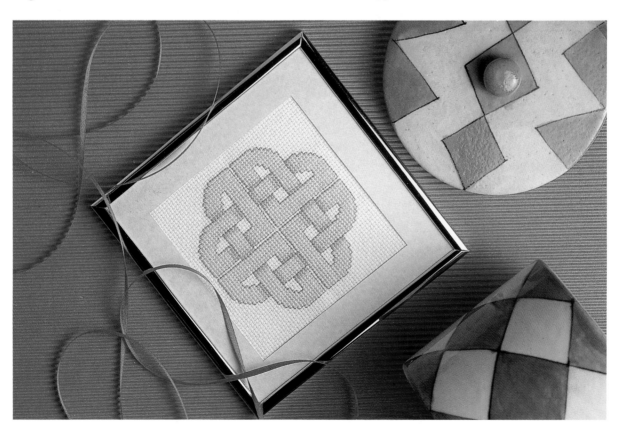

4 Press the embroidery from the back (see page 10). Trim the fabric to the required size, then follow the instructions on the frame for mounting and assembling the picture.

VARIATIONS

This versatile knot shape can be used in many different ways. Work it on smaller-gauge fabric as a greetings card, or use the waste canvas method (see page 10) to work it on a sweatshirt or blouse pocket.

Because the design is made up of heart shapes, it would look effective stitched in shades of pink as a wedding or Valentine's Day card. Try using DMC 3716, 962 and 961, or Anchor 74, 75 and 76, outlined with red or silver metallic thread.

PRACTICAL TIP

If you want to hang the finished picture diagonally, as shown here, you will need to position the hanging ring of the frame at one corner.

KEY			
DMC 742	Anchor 303	●	Dark yellow
DMC 743	Anchor 302	•	Mid-yellow
DMC 744	Anchor 301	0	Light yellow
Your chosen gold thread		–	

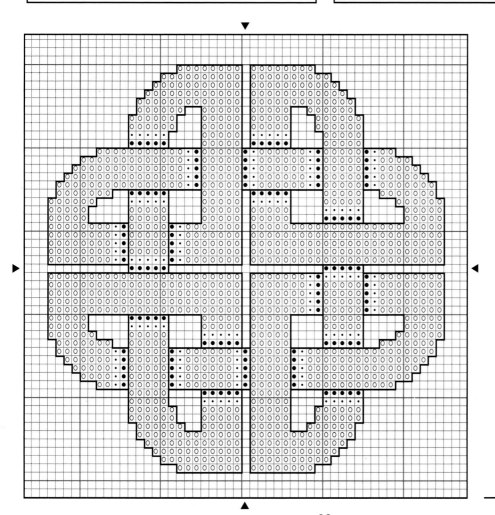

EMBROIDERED CHRISTENING ROBE

A special occasion calls for a special garment; this christening robe is decorated with a Celtic knotwork border design on the bodice, with single motifs on the sleeves, back yokes and skirt.

Stitch count: border 19 x 73, motif 19 x 37
Design size: border 7 x 2in (18 x 5cm)
motif 4 x 2in (10 x 5cm)

MATERIALS
- One pattern for a christening robe
- White, ivory or cream silk fabric, as required by the pattern
- Waste canvas, 11hpi, 1/4yd (20cm)
- White lining fabric, buttons, thread, etc, as required by the pattern
- Three skeins of stranded cotton: DMC white or Anchor 1
- One spool of silver embroidery thread, such as Madeira No 40, silver
- Medium crewel needle
- Tacking (basting) thread

PRODUCING THE DESIGN
1 Lay out the pattern pieces on the silk fabric to check their layout. Cut out the skirt pieces and keep to one side; for the yoke pieces

and sleeves, tack (baste) the outlines onto single layers of silk and then remove the pattern pieces.

2 Cut a piece of waste canvas (see page 10) so that it fits the width of the front yoke inside the seam allowances; it needs to be 21 squares deep. Find and mark its centre line, then tack (baste) the strip of waste canvas in position on the right side of the front yoke area marked on your fabric.

3 Using three strands of white thread, and beginning at the centre of the design and working outwards, stitch the border design onto the front yoke.

4 Cut five rectangles of waste canvas, 40 squares long and 21 squares wide. Tack (baste) one on each of the back yoke shapes marked on your fabric, making sure that they are level and within the seam allowances. Tack (baste) one on the centre line of each sleeve about half-way down, and one on the centre front of the skirt 6-8in (15-20cm) up from the bottom.

5 Using three strands of white thread, stitch the smaller motif onto each of the five rectangles of waste canvas.

6 Follow the instructions on page 55 to remove the waste canvas. Leave the pieces of silk to dry, held on a large embroidery frame secured outside the pattern areas to prevent the silk from puckering.

7 Keeping the fabric on the embroidery frame and using two strands of silver thread, outline the knot designs with back stitch (see page 9), as shown on the charts.

8 Cut the pattern pieces out of the silk along the tacked (basted) lines, then make up the robe, following the instructions given with the pattern.

PRACTICAL TIP

Remove the waste canvas before you work the back stitches (see page 10), otherwise the silver thread may catch some of the canvas threads and make them difficult to remove.

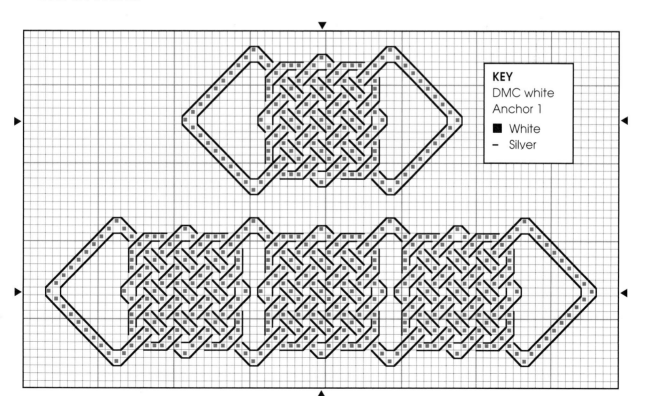

KEY
DMC white
Anchor 1
■ White
– Silver

SQUARE CUSHION

The Celts produced knotwork patterns that could fill any shape, whether regular or irregular. The design for this cushion began as a right-angled triangular knot; I have combined four identical knots and made the lines of the different sections flow into each other to form a square.

Stitch count: 111 x 111
Design size: 20 x 20in (51 x 51cm)

MATERIALS

- One piece of cream or grey binca, 6hpi, 25½in (65cm) square
- Anchor tapestry yarn in the colours given in the key
- Large tapestry needle
- Two rectangles of thick, firm grey fabric such as sailcloth or twill, 16 x 22in (40 x 55cm)
- One reel of grey sewing thread
- Cushion pad

PRODUCING THE DESIGN

1 Fold the binca in half lengthwise and press the fold lightly, then fold it in half widthways and press. Where the two folds meet is the centre of your fabric and will be the centre of your design; mark it with a pin or a dot of water-soluble pen.
2 Beginning at the centre of the fabric and the chart, stitch all the very dark aqua outline stitches as marked on the chart.
3 When the outlines are complete, stitch the dark aqua and mid-aqua stitches as marked on the chart.
4 Fill in all the other squares within the outlines with the pale aqua; as the outlines are already in position, there is no need to count the squares.

5 Using dark grey, stitch a few isolated squares at random across the background inside and outside the knot design (the background extends three squares beyond the outermost parts of the knot).
6 Using mid-grey, stitch a few more isolated stitches at random in the same way across the same parts.
7 Using light grey, fill in all the remaining parts of the background.
8 When all the embroidery is complete, press the design from the back (see page 10). Trim the edges of the binca to within ³/4in (2cm) all around.
9 Turn under, press and stitch a small double hem on one long side of each rectangle of grey fabric. Lay the embroidery face up on a flat surface, then lay the two grey rectangles, right sides down, on top, overlapping them so that their edges line up with the raw edges of the binca.
10 Pin and tack (baste) along the line made by the very edge of the embroidery, then stitch around this line by machine twice, going over the corners several times to reinforce them. Clip the corners and trim the seams back to 3in (7.5cm). Turn the cover to the right side, pushing the corners out with the head of a bodkin or knitting needle, and press from the back (see page 10).

PRACTICAL TIP

You don't need to follow the exact squares marked on the chart for the different greys; just scatter the dark grey and mid-grey stitches at random, as described in the instructions, then fill in the rest with light grey. If you choose alternative colours for your cushion, follow the same instructions using your choice of three background shades.

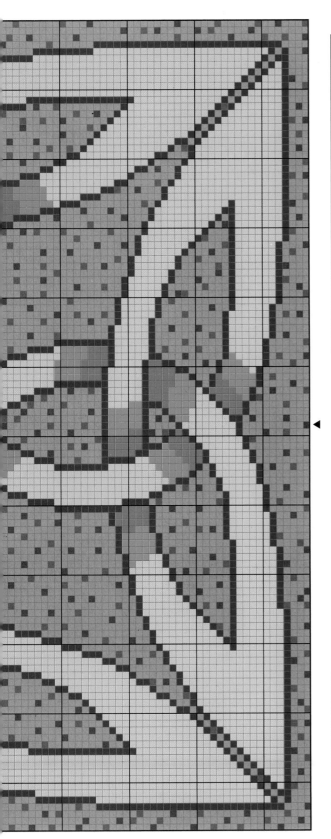

VARIATIONS

This design would look equally effective in different colourways; try picking out colours from your own décor. Make sure that you buy the right number of skeins of each shade; the greatest number of skeins is needed of the palest background colour and the palest colour inside the knot, and seven skeins are needed of the colour you choose for the outlines.

Because this design is stitched in yarn, it will be very hard-wearing; you could use it for chair-seats and upholstered chair-backs as well as for cushions.

KEY	SKEINS		
Anchor 9786	14	▦	Light grey
Anchor 9790	2	▦	Mid-grey
Anchor 9794	2	▦	Dark grey
Anchor 8914	12	▦	Light aqua
Anchor 8918	2	▦	Mid-aqua
Anchor 8920	2	▦	Dark aqua
Anchor 8922	7	▦	Very dark aqua

ANIMALS AND PEOPLE

Living creatures of all kinds feature frequently in Celtic art. Perhaps best known are the quaint birds, their down-turned beaks often giving them a baleful look. The birds come in all shapes and sizes, and although they are sometimes recognisable as a particular species – perhaps a duck or a peacock – they are generally adorned with elaborate stylised plumage. Fish are rarely depicted in Celtic art, although when they do appear, they get much the same stylised treatment as the birds, with their scales illustrated in the same patterns.

Even more extraordinary are the unrecognisable reptilian creatures which are often incorporated into elaborate knots: the serpents on page 48 are a legacy of this fashion. Celtic artists also had a fondness for depicting animals that were part-horse and part-seahorse, with

equine heads and vaguely horse-like legs, but with very long bodies which also occasionally had fins! The design on page 122 shows some of these creatures. Animals such as lions, of which presumably the artists had never seen reliable pictures, gave rise to some very strange and fantastic creatures similar to the lion-dogs of Imperial Chinese art; the picture on page 46 features a Celtic lion.

Other creatures, however, were illustrated with more realism by Celtic artists; their depictions of horses, boars, deer and dogs were often surprisingly fresh. Humans and angels had mixed fortunes: some were realistic, some beautiful, while others were ugly enough to pass for gargoyles. The projects on the following pages reflect the different Celtic styles in portraying living creatures, from the simple and realistic to the fantastic.

ḥORSE CARD AND PICTURE

The same basic design is used here for the card and the picture (shown on page 6). The card is worked small, in *petit point* on grey even-weave fabric, using just the horse's outline; the picture is a mirror image, with the outline stitched in the same dark turquoise on a white background but filled with paler turquoise.

Stitch count: 84 x 69
Design size: picture 6 x 5in (15.5 x 13cm) card 3¹/2 x 3in (9 x 7.5cm)

MATERIALS
For the picture you will need:
- One piece of white Aida, 14hpi, 10in (25cm) square
- Stranded cottons (floss) in the colours given in the key

- Fine tapestry needle
- Frame to fit the finished picture, with an aperture at least 7in (18cm) square

For the card you will need:
- One piece of grey even-weave fabric, approximately 25hpi, 6in (15cm) square
- Stranded cotton (floss) in the colour given in the key
- Very fine tapestry needle
- White card blank with an aperture at least 3¹/2in (8.5cm) square

PRODUCING THE DESIGNS
To make the picture:
1 Measure in 2in (5cm) from the right-hand side of the fabric and 2¹/2in (6cm) down from the top; this point is where you will begin stitching and corresponds to the tip of the horse's ear.
2 Using two strands of dark turquoise, stitch the outline of the horse following the chart. Using two strands of light turquoise, fill in all the areas inside the horse.
3 Press the embroidery from the back on a clean, soft surface (see page 10), then mount in the frame, following the manufacturer's instructions.

To make the card:
1 Measure in 1¹/2in (4cm) from the left-hand edge of the fabric and 1³/4in (4.5cm) down from the top; this point is where you will begin stitching and corresponds to the tip of the horse's ear.
2 Using one strand of dark turquoise, follow the chart to stitch the outlines of the horse.
3 Press the embroidery from the back (see page 10), then follow the instructions on page 71 for mounting it in the card blank.

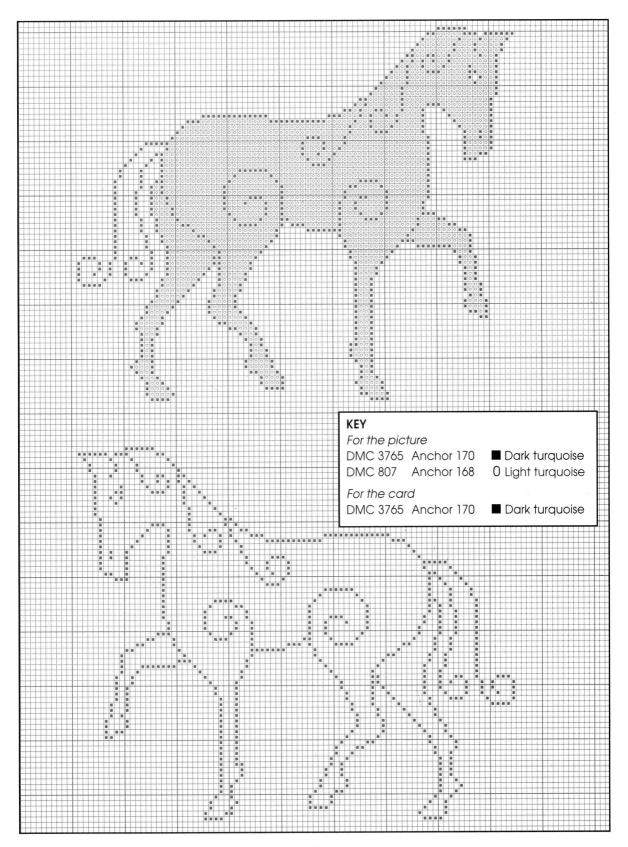

KEY
For the picture
DMC 3765   Anchor 170   ■ Dark turquoise
DMC 807   Anchor 168   0 Light turquoise

For the card
DMC 3765   Anchor 170   ■ Dark turquoise

BABY'S BIB

Ducks are always favourite animals to decorate baby items, and here a little detail from a Celtic manuscript has been turned into a design to adorn a baby's bib. The original had a head and neck outline made from white dots on a brown background; I have achieved the same effect with alternate squares of dark and light colours. If you wish, add some of the ducklings from page 41.

Stitch count: 50 x 39
Design size: 4 x 3in (10 x 7.5cm)

MATERIALS

- One baby's bib suitable for cross stitch
- Stranded cottons (floss) in the colours given in the key
- Medium tapestry needle
- Water soluble pen for marking

PRODUCING THE DESIGN

1 Measure up $1\frac{1}{2}$in (4cm) from the bottom of the bib, and draw a line across the fabric of the bib in water-soluble pen at this level. This line will mark the bottom of your stitching, and corresponds to the line marked on the chart.

2 Using two strands of brown, stitch the squares marked as the dark outlines on the chart. Begin with the front foot, starting it on the marked line $2\frac{1}{2}$in (6cm) in from the left-hand edge.

3 Using two strands of cotton (floss) throughout, stitch the coloured portions of the chart as marked. Count the squares carefully from the duck's feet to the reeds, and stitch those following the chart.

4 Using one strand of brown, work back stitch (see page 9) around all the edges of the squares marked for back stitch.

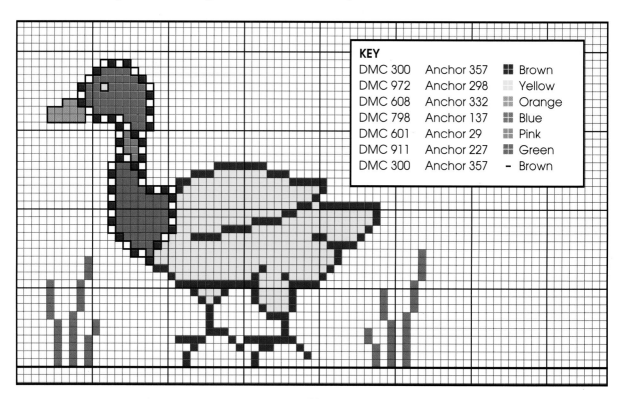

KEY			
DMC 300	Anchor 357	▦	Brown
DMC 972	Anchor 298	▦	Yellow
DMC 608	Anchor 332	▦	Orange
DMC 798	Anchor 137	▦	Blue
DMC 601	Anchor 29	▦	Pink
DMC 911	Anchor 227	▦	Green
DMC 300	Anchor 357	–	Brown

VARIATION
This duck is so much fun that you might want to stitch a parade of them on a cross-stitch band to march across a pram quilt or a cot bumper; use the chart below as a guide, and add as many ducklings as you wish.

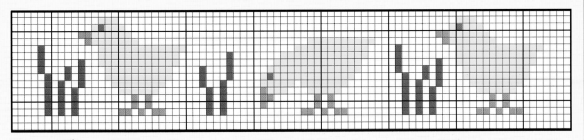

PEACOCK WAISTCOAT

Bright peacocks decorate this flamboyant waistcoat; the same design is worked on each front panel, but as a mirror image. Although the area covered is large, thick soft cotton threads and large-gauge canvas mean that the work grows quickly.

Stitch count: 60 x 88
Design size: 15 x 10in (38 x 26cm)

MATERIALS

For an adult-sized waistcoat, you will need:

- A waistcoat pattern with simple front pieces
- Two pieces of cream binca, 6hpi, the size of your waistcoat front pattern piece
- Soft cottons in the colours given in the key
- Large tapestry needle
- Thick cream calico (muslin) fabric (you will need the amount stipulated for the waistcoat and lining on your pattern)
- Matching sewing thread
- Iron-on fusing web, two pieces to fit your pieces of binca
- Tacking (basting) thread

PRODUCING THE DESIGN

1 Press the binca. Cut out the paper pattern piece for your waistcoat front and trace one side in each direction onto the binca, using a water-soluble pen. Tack (baste) around these lines to mark the pattern shapes.

2 Count the squares of binca covered by the pattern piece, and check that the peacock design will fit onto the binca pieces and still allow for the seams. If not, adjust your pattern piece slightly to take in the design. Using a water-soluble pen, mark the places on the binca where the designs need to go so that they fit into the shapes and are level with

each other; the best way to do this is to mark the level and position of the peacock's feet on each design.

3 Using black, follow the charts to stitch the design outlines onto the binca, beginning from the areas you have marked. If you have marked the fabric correctly, the peacock designs will fall within your tacked (basted) pattern areas on each piece of binca.

4 Fill in the solid areas in the appropriate colours as marked on the charts.

5 Using black, work back stitch (see page 9) around the edges of the pink squares on each peacock's tail.

6 Sponge away any marks left by the water-soluble pen; when the embroideries are completely dry, iron them from the back (see page 10), pulling the binca back square if it has become slightly distorted. Lay the pieces of fusing web, web side down, on the backs of the embroideries, and iron them to fuse them to the fabric. Cut around the tacked (basted) lines marking the edges of the pattern pieces.

7 From the calico, use your pattern to cut the waistcoat back and fronts and the lining back and fronts. Peel the backing paper away from the web on the embroideries; lay the embroideries face down and position the calico waistcoat fronts on top, then iron to fuse the calico to the web. You now have two embroidered waistcoat fronts; make up the waistcoat as instructed in the pattern.

PRACTICAL TIP

When you are checking that the peacock design fits your waistcoat pattern, try the peacocks out back-to-back as well as face-to-face; the design may fit your waistcoat more easily that way.

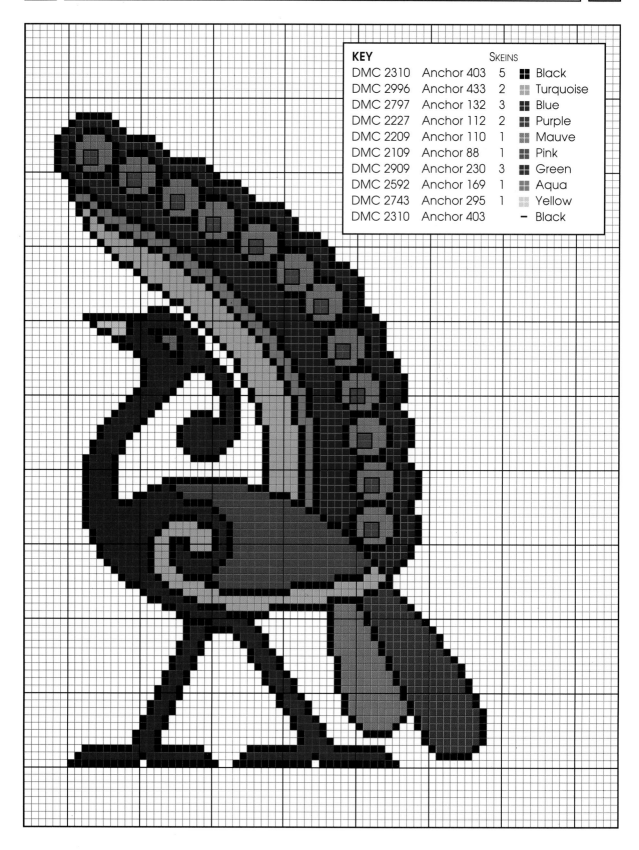

KEY		Skeins		
DMC 2310	Anchor 403	5		Black
DMC 2996	Anchor 433	2		Turquoise
DMC 2797	Anchor 132	3		Blue
DMC 2227	Anchor 112	2		Purple
DMC 2209	Anchor 110	1		Mauve
DMC 2109	Anchor 88	1		Pink
DMC 2909	Anchor 230	3		Green
DMC 2592	Anchor 169	1		Aqua
DMC 2743	Anchor 295	1		Yellow
DMC 2310	Anchor 403		−	Black

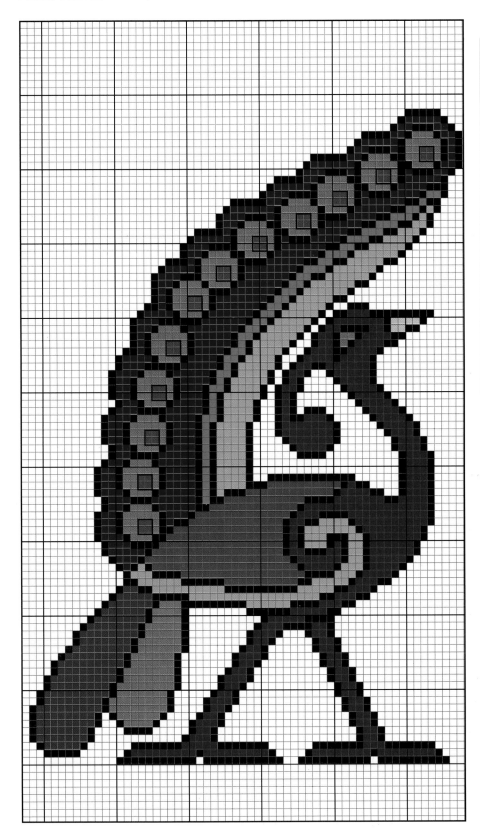

VARIATION

If you want to adapt the peacock design for a child's pattern, use a smaller-gauge canvas (such as 8 or 11hpi Aida), and a finer thread such as coton perlé. As with the adult waistcoat, trace out the pattern and count the squares of the fabric to make sure that it will fit it.

LION PICTURE

Serocious mythical beasts, such as the bizarre creatures that were half-lion, half-dog, were often depicted by Celtic artists. This roundel features a brightly coloured version of just such a creature.

Stitch count: 62 x 52
Design size: 4¹/₂ x 4in (11.5 x 10cm)

MATERIALS
- One piece of white Aida fabric, 14hpi, at least 8in (20cm) square
- Stranded cottons (floss) in the colours given in the key
- Medium tapestry needle

- One circular wooden picture frame with a 4³/₄-5in (12-13cm) opening

PRODUCING THE DESIGN
1 Measure 1¹/₂in (4cm) from the left-hand side of your square of fabric and 3in (7.5cm) down from the top; mark this point with a dot of water-soluble pen. This will be your starting point for stitching.
2 The marked dot corresponds to the tip of the lion's nose. Using two strands of black, begin working at the marked point and stitch all the black outlines marked on the chart.
3 Using two strands of cotton (floss) throughout, fill in the different parts of the lion with the colours marked on the chart.

4 When the embroidery is complete, remove the dot of pen with a damp cloth; when the fabric is completely dry, press it from the back (see page 10).

5 Trim the fabric into a circle to fit the frame, and assemble the embroidery and frame according to the manufacturer's instructions.

VARIATIONS

The lion design looks outstanding in these bold, stained-glass colours; if you want to soften its appearance a little, try choosing mid-blue for the outline and gentler shades for the filled areas.

In contrast, if you want to make the design more visually striking, work the outlines in black, or gold, and work the colours in one strand of stranded cotton (floss) and one strand of a bright metallic thread.

Embroider the lion as a crest on a blazer pocket, using the waste canvas method (see page 10), or work a matching pair as bookmarks or coaster designs.

KEY			
DMC 608	Anchor 332	▦	Orange
DMC 702	Anchor 226	▦	Green
DMC 796	Anchor 133	▦	Blue
DMC 602	Anchor 63	▦	Pink
DMC 552	Anchor 112	▦	Purple
DMC 3765	Anchor 170	▦	Aqua
DMC 972	Anchor 298	▦	Yellow
DMC 310	Anchor 403	▦	Black

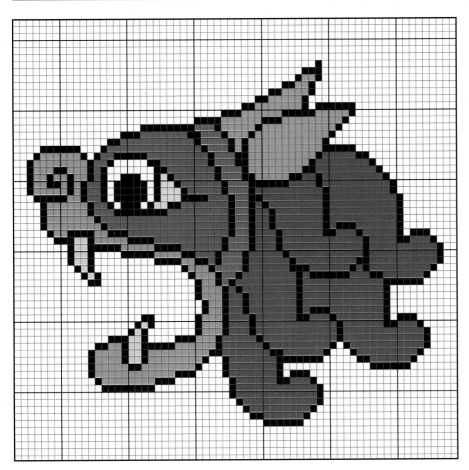

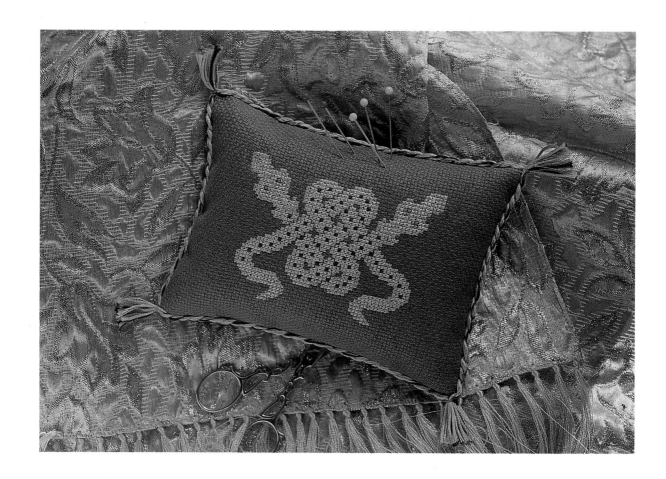

SERPENT PINCUSHION

Many Celtic designs combined knotwork with strange, elongated snouted reptiles, which are not immediately recognisable as any specific animal! The design for this pincushion echoes that favourite combination.

Stitch count: 57 x 41
Design size: 4 x 3in (10 x 8cm)

MATERIALS
- Two pieces of dark blue Aida, 14hpi, 6 x 8in (15 x 20cm)
- Two pieces of iron-on stiffening fabric, 6 x 8in (15 x 20cm)
- Stranded cottons (floss) in the colours given in the key
- Matching blue sewing thread

- One spool of fine gold thread, such as Madeira No 40, gold 7
- Fine tapestry needle
- White or pale blue crayon for marking
- Stuffing

PRODUCING THE DESIGN
1 Fold one of the pieces of blue fabric lengthwise and press gently, then fold it widthways and press. Put a dot of crayon where the folds meet; this is the centre of your work, and will correspond to the dark blue stitch in the very middle of the serpent design.
2 Using two strands of dark yellow and one strand of gold, follow the chart and work all the outline stitches of the design.
3 Using two strands of the appropriate colour

for all the other cross stitches, follow the chart to stitch the rest of the design.

4 Using one strand of dark blue, work back stitch (see page 9) where marked on the chart – where the serpents cross over themselves or each other, and around the orange stitches that form the pupils of the eyes.

5 Press the embroidery from the back (see page 10). Position the pieces of stiffening fabric on the backs of the blue fabric pieces and fuse the layers together with an iron.

6 Place the two pieces of blue fabric right sides together; pin, tack and machine stitch around three sides of the rectangle, taking a 1/2in (12mm) seam. Clip the corners and trim the seam allowances, and turn the shape to the right side.

7 Turn under and press the seam allowance of 1/2in (12mm) on the raw edge. Fill the pincushion firmly with the stuffing, then stitch the turned edges together with ladder stitch or overcasting.

8 From the remaining embroidery threads, cut several strands about 2yd (2m) long of each colour. Put them all together and tie one end of the hank to a firm object such as a door handle; twist the threads together firmly, then double them back on themselves to make a stable length of cord.

9 Leaving 3/4-1 1/4in (2-3cm) of the hank free at one end, begin stitching the cord to one side of the pincushion. Cut the cord with 3/4-1 1/4in (2-3cm) free at the other end, then repeat with the other three sides of the pincushion. Work a few tight stitches around the tops of the free bits of cord to create a tassel, then cut the ends off to even lengths.

KEY			
DMC 743	Anchor 302	■	Dark yellow + Gold
DMC 745	Anchor 301	\	Pale yellow
DMC 797	Anchor 147	▲	Dark blue
DMC 334	Anchor 145	0	Mid-blue
DMC 3325	Anchor 144	+	Light blue
DMC 970	Anchor 324	•	Orange
DMC 797	Anchor 147	-	Dark blue

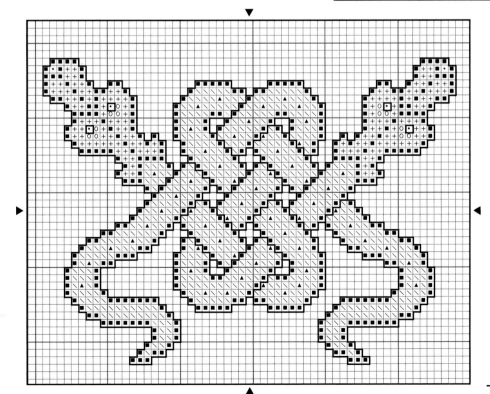

STAINED-GLASS ANGEL

Exotic saints and angels fill Celtic illuminations; this Christmas design was inspired by several different figures. The black outlines and jewel-like colours make the design glow like a piece of stained glass.

Stitch count: 112 x 183
Design size: 17 x 11in (43 x 28cm)

MATERIALS

- One piece of white Aida, 11hpi, 26 x 16in (65 x 40cm)
- Stranded cottons (floss) in the colours given in the key
- One spool of gold thread such as Gütermann metallic 24
- Medium tapestry needle
- Frame to fit the finished picture

PRODUCING THE DESIGN

1 Fold the fabric in half and press gently to give a mid-line from top to bottom. Measure 4³/₄in (12cm) down this line from the top edge of the fabric, and make a dot with a water-soluble pen.

2 Using three strands of black, begin stitching at the dot; the dot corresponds to the middle of the top line of the halo. Stitch all the black outlines as marked on the chart, and the 'PAX' within the rectangular panel.

3 Using two strands of yellow and one strand of gold thread, stitch the areas marked as yellow on the chart: the staff, the halo and the outside border of the rectagular panel.

4 Using three strands of the appropriate colours, stitch all the remaining areas of the design as marked on the chart. Using one strand of brown, work the nose, eyebrows, chin and eye outlines in back stitch (see

page 9) as marked on the chart.

5 When the embroidery is complete, sponge away the mark from the water-soluble pen; leave the fabric to dry completely, then iron it from the back (see page 10).

6 Assemble the frame and/or mount according to the manufacturer's instructions.

PRACTICAL TIP
When you are choosing your threads for this project, stick to either DMC or Anchor throughout; occasionally the colours do not correspond exactly across the brands, so if you mix them the shades may not blend quite so well.

The halo and staff have a strand of gold worked with the yellow thread

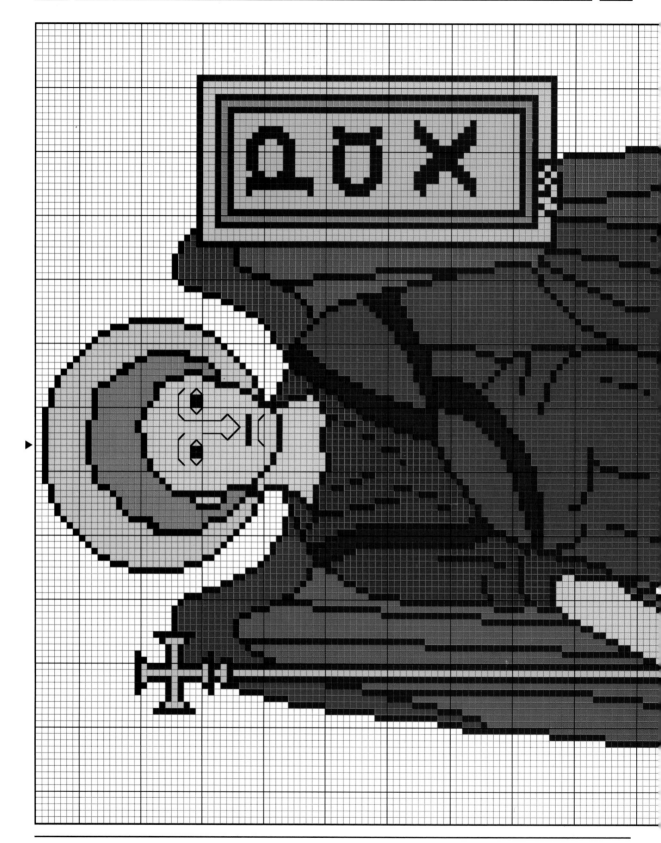

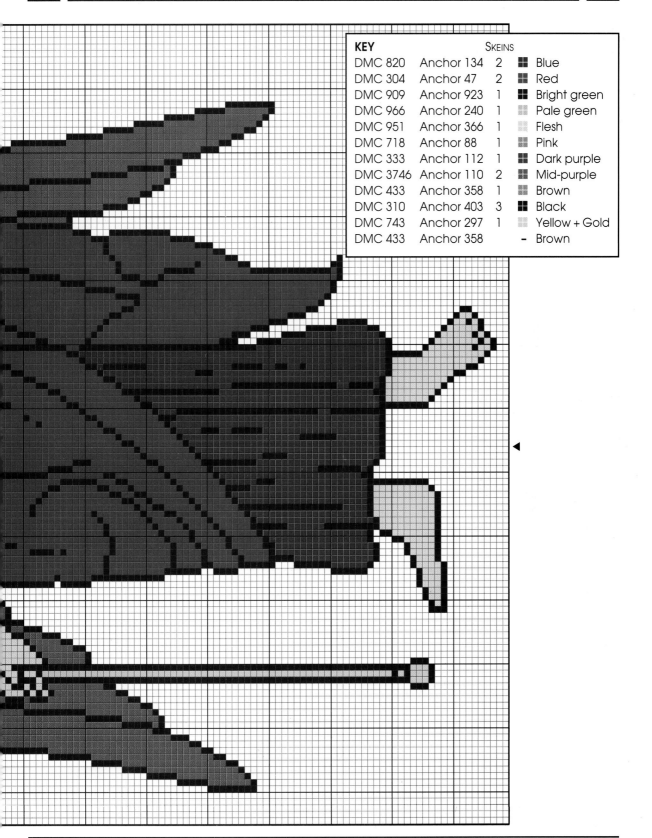

KEY		SKEINS		
DMC 820	Anchor 134	2	▦	Blue
DMC 304	Anchor 47	2	▦	Red
DMC 909	Anchor 923	1	▦	Bright green
DMC 966	Anchor 240	1	▦	Pale green
DMC 951	Anchor 366	1	▦	Flesh
DMC 718	Anchor 88	1	▦	Pink
DMC 333	Anchor 112	1	▦	Dark purple
DMC 3746	Anchor 110	2	▦	Mid-purple
DMC 433	Anchor 358	1	▦	Brown
DMC 310	Anchor 403	3	▦	Black
DMC 743	Anchor 297	1	▦	Yellow + Gold
DMC 433	Anchor 358		–	Brown

COCKEREL SWEATSHIRT

Brighten up a plain sweatshirt with a quirky Celtic bird; the design is stitched using waste canvas as a guide, so you can stitch it onto any sweatshirt or sweater – or even a T-shirt!

Stitch count: 54 x 48
Design size: 5$\frac{1}{4}$ x 5$\frac{1}{4}$in (13.5 x 13.5cm)

MATERIALS
- Dark blue sweatshirt
- Piece of waste canvas, 11hpi, at least 6$\frac{1}{4}$in (16cm) square
- Stranded cottons (floss) in the colours given in the key
- Medium-sized crewel needle
- Tacking (basting) thread

PRODUCING THE DESIGN
1 Decide on the position of your motif; its finished size is 5$\frac{1}{4}$in (13.5cm) square, so this will help you to see the space that it will take up on the background. When you have decided on the position, tack (baste) the piece of waste canvas onto the sweatshirt to cover the area.
2 Using three strands of cotton (floss), stitch the design, following the colours marked on the chart. Take each stitch across one double thread of the waste canvas (see page 10), down the hole in the canvas and into the fabric behind. Make sure that each stitch goes into the background fabric. Stitch the blue outlines of the bird first, so that you do not need to count the stitches inside the outlines.

3 When the stitching is complete, dampen the whole design with a sponge and a little warm water; this dissolves the glue holding the canvas threads together.

4 When the glue has dissolved, pull the threads of the canvas out from under the stitches. You may find it useful to use tweezers for this task. Once all the threads have been removed you will be left with the embroidered design on a plain background; allow it to dry, then press the design from the back with a steam iron (see page 10).

PRACTICAL TIP

Try not to pull the stitches too tight as you are working over the waste canvas; if you leave them a little loose, it will be easier to pull the canvas threads out later.

VARIATIONS

The waste canvas method (see page 10) allows you to work counted thread designs onto virtually any background; you could try this design on a pocket or a blouse-front, or work it onto a plain fabric for an egg-cosy.

Pairs of birds would look good on the corners of curtains or the ends of a table runner; just flip the chart from left to right for a mirror image.

Of course, you don't have to use waste canvas for this design; it can be stitched on Aida for a simple card, or worked large for a bright cushion.

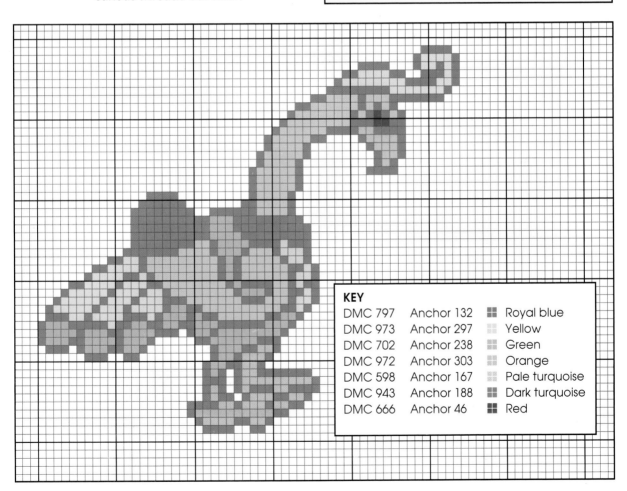

KEY			
DMC 797	Anchor 132	▦	Royal blue
DMC 973	Anchor 297	▦	Yellow
DMC 702	Anchor 238	▦	Green
DMC 972	Anchor 303	▦	Orange
DMC 598	Anchor 167	▦	Pale turquoise
DMC 943	Anchor 188	▦	Dark turquoise
DMC 666	Anchor 46	▦	Red

CURTAIN TIE-BACK

S ish appear occasionally in Celtic art, usually as highly stylised and decorative features. The curving fish motif on this design fits perfectly the curve of the curtain tie-back.

Stitch count: 123 x 75
Design size: 9 x 5½in (23 x 14cm)

MATERIALS
For each pair of tie-backs you will need:
- Paper and pencil to enlarge the design
- One piece of moss green Aida, 14hpi, 28 x 20in (70 x 50cm)
- One piece of firm iron-on stiffening fabric, the same size
- One piece of matching green cotton backing fabric, the same size
- Two skeins of stranded cotton (floss) in DMC White or Anchor 1
- Fine tapestry needle
- 3yd (3m) matching green bias binding, ½in (12mm) wide
- Four large curtain rings
- Tacking thread
- Matching sewing thread

PRODUCING THE DESIGN
1 Enlarge the tie-back outline to the correct size and cut out the shape. Using this as a guide, cut two shapes from the stiffening fabric and two from the backing fabric.
2 Trace the shape twice onto the green Aida using a water-soluble pen. On one shape, measure ½in (12mm) to the right of the central line and 2in (5cm) up from the bottom; mark the position with a dot of water-soluble pen. On the other shape, measure ½in (12mm) to the left of the central line and 2in (5cm) up, and mark this

position in the same way. On each of the fish charts you will see that there is a vertical line of four cross stitches at the tip of the head. The bottom stitch of the four will correspond with the dot marked on the fabric.
3 Using two strands of white cotton (floss) throughout, and beginning at the marked dots, stitch the designs onto the fabric.
4 When the stitching is complete, the fish shapes should sit comfortably within the marked outlines. (If by any chance they do not, redraw the outlines slightly to accommodate them.) Cut out the fabric shapes around the marked outlines. Sponge away the marked dots and allow the fabric to dry completely, then press from the back (see page 10).
5 Lay each embroidery face down, and position a piece of stiffening fabric, adhesive side down, on top; fuse the layers together by ironing.
6 Lay the two pieces of backing fabric, right side down, on a flat surface. Cover each piece with one of the embroideries, right side up. Pin and tack (baste) the bias binding face down around the edges of each piece, aligning the raw edges, then stitch along the line by machine. Fold the free edge of the binding over the raw fabric edges, tuck it under and slip stitch the binding to the back of each tie-back.
7 Stitch a curtain ring to the back of each end of both tie-backs with a few strong overcasting stitches.

PRACTICAL TIP
Don't cut the fabric shapes out of the Aida before you embroider them; if you leave it until the stitching is done the edges will not fray and lose their definition.

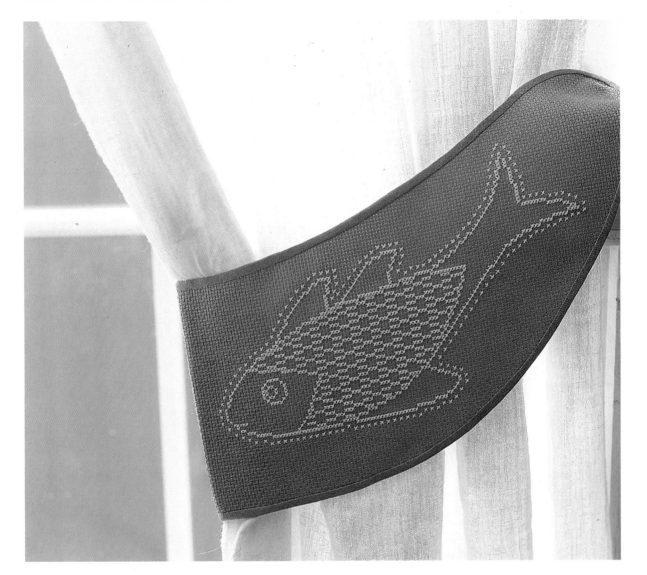

24in (60cm)

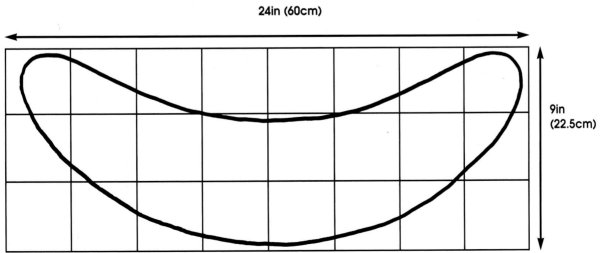

9in
(22.5cm)

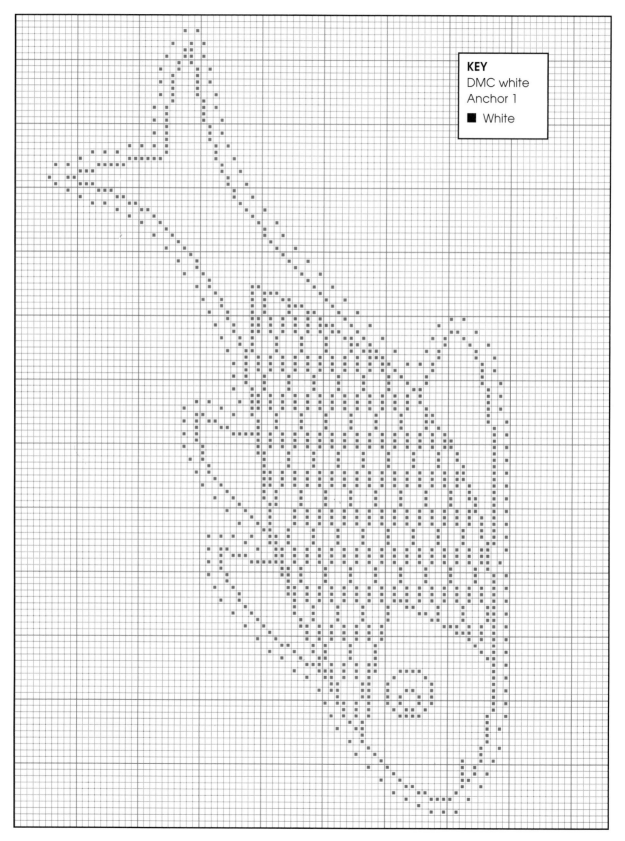

KEY
DMC white
Anchor 1
■ White

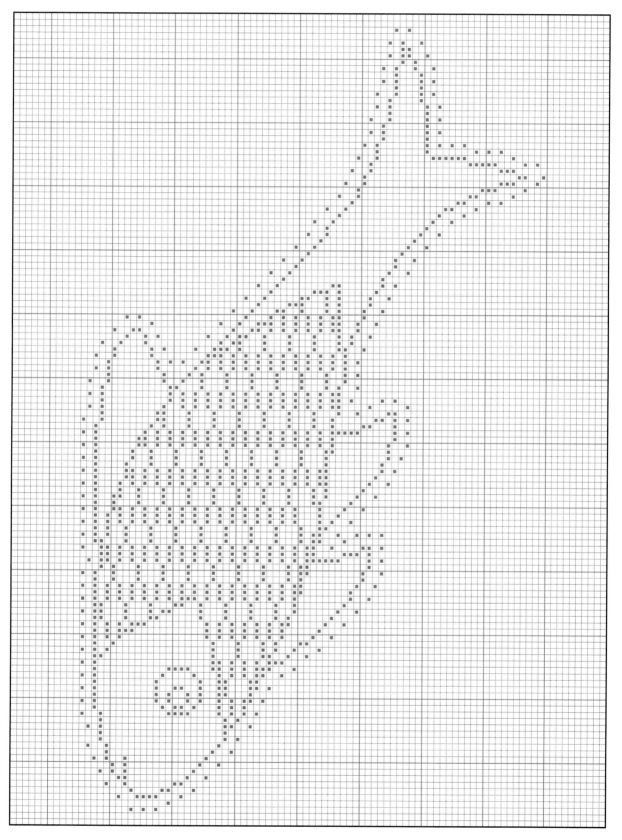

ḞORSEMAN PICTURE

W̲hen horsemen appear in Celtic designs they are usually depicted realistically, dressed in simple clothing and armed with a basic sword and shield. This panel combines a realistic horse and rider with cross-topped columns taken from the borders of a carpet page; the colours are from the more subtle range of the Celtic palette.

Stitch count: 196 x 112
Design size: 14 x 8in (36 x 20cm)

MATERIALS
- One piece of cream Aida, 14hpi, 18 x 12in (45 x 30cm)
- Stranded cottons (floss) in the colours given in the key
- One spool of fairly thick silver embroidery thread such as Gütermann metallic 41
- Fine tapestry needle
- Frame to fit the finished picture, with an aperture at least 16 x 10in (40 x 25cm)

PRODUCING THE DESIGN
1 Press the Aida. Measure up 2in (5cm) from the bottom of the fabric and draw a horizontal line in water-soluble pen at that level. This will be the baseline which you will use as a guide for positioning the design.
2 Measure in 2in (5cm) along this line from the edge of the fabric (measure in from whichever edge you prefer to start), and make a dot with the water-soluble pen. The dot is the place where you will start stitching and marks the outside edge of the dark pink base of the cross.
3 Using two strands of cotton (floss) in the appropriate colours, follow the chart to stitch the cross at the side you have marked. When

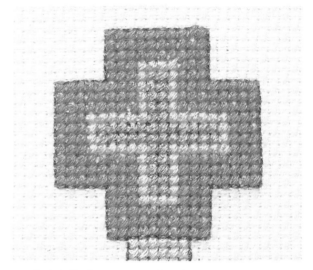

A detail of one cross, showing the back stitch outlines around the coloured areas

the cross is complete, outline the different parts of it with back stitch (see page 9) in one strand of dark brown cotton, as marked on the chart.
4 Count the squares of fabric carefully to see where to position the horse in relation to your stitched cross. Work all the dark brown outlines of the horse and rider next, and then work the horseman's beard, which is in the same colour.
5 Using the appropriate colours, fill in all the solid areas of the horse and rider. Use one strand of dark brown to outline the horseman's eye and the circles on the shield.
6 Stitch the second cross in position, then finish it off with back stitch in the same way as the first.
7 When the embroidery is complete, sponge away the marks made by the water-soluble pen; when it is completely dry, press the embroidery from the back (see page 10), then mount in your chosen frame, following the manufacturer's instructions.

PRACTICAL TIP

Many colours are needed for this horseman and for most of them only a small amount of thread is used; if you have a good selection of stranded cottons (floss) from previous projects, you may be able to use some of them as substitutes for the colours listed — try them out together to check that they harmonise before you stitch with them.

KEY

DMC	Anchor		Colour
DMC 610	Anchor 375	▓▓	Dark brown
DMC 611	Anchor 374	▓▓	Mid-brown
DMC 3828	Anchor 943	▓▓	Light brown
DMC 739	Anchor 956	░░	Beige
DMC 561	Anchor 218	▓▓	Dark green
DMC 562	Anchor 216	▓▓	Mid-green
DMC 564	Anchor 214	▓▓	Light green
DMC 471	Anchor 265	▓▓	Lime green
DMC 824	Anchor 147	▓▓	Dark blue
DMC 3755	Anchor 978	▓▓	Mid-blue
DMC 775	Anchor 976	▓▓	Light blue
DMC 3350	Anchor 69	▓▓	Dark pink
DMC 3354	Anchor 66	░░	Light pink
DMC 333	Anchor 873	▓▓	Dark purple
DMC 340	Anchor 871	▓▓	Light purple
DMC 920	Anchor 339	▓▓	Rust
DMC 783	Anchor 890	░░	Light rust
DMC 951	Anchor 942	░░	Flesh
DMC 415	Anchor 398	▓▓	Grey
		░░	Silver
DMC 610	Anchor 375	–	Dark brown

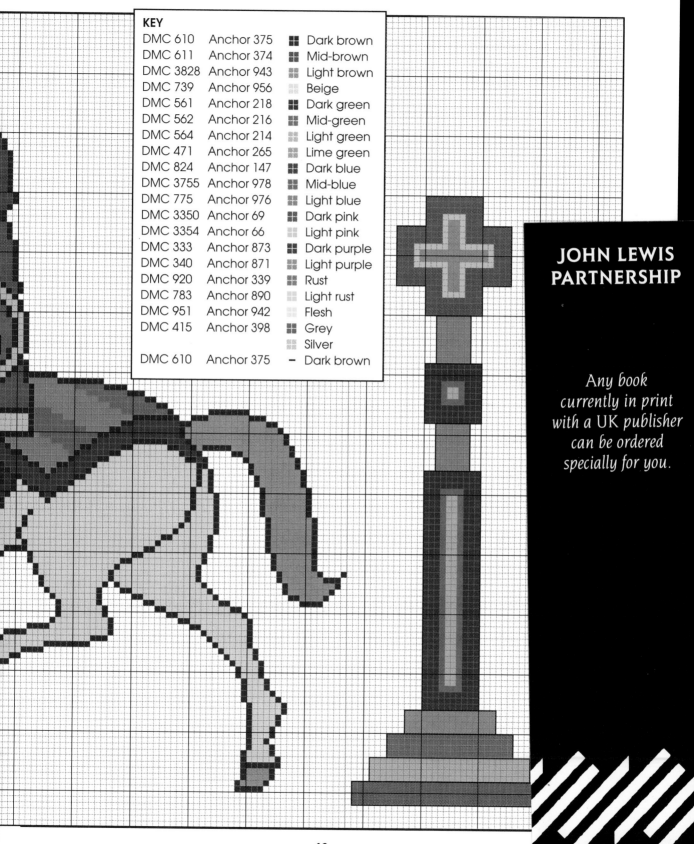

63

CELTIC RUG

Birds and knotwork are combined in this striking design. Although this is the largest project in the book, it is not as time-consuming as it looks as the stitching is in double knitting yarn on large-gauge canvas.

Stitch count: 259 x 187
Design size: 45 x 31in (115 x 79cm)

MATERIALS

- One piece of cream binca, 6hpi, 3¹/4 x 4¹/2ft (1m x 1m 40cm)
- 100g balls of double knitting yarn in the colours given in the key
- Large tapestry needle
- One piece of firm backing fabric, such as linen or thick calico (muslin), the same size as the binca
- Matching sewing thread

PRODUCING THE DESIGN

1 Fold the fabric in half along its length and mark the line with a water-soluble pen. This will act as a stitching guide for the different parts of the design.

2 Measure in 6in (15cm) from one end of the fabric and mark a line with the water-soluble pen. The edges of the first two knotwork borders will lie along this line. Using one strand of dark blue, begin stitching the two knotwork border outlines at this end of the fabric, making sure that you leave one empty square between them. When the outlines of the first two knotwork borders are complete, stitch the outlines of the other two, again leaving one empty square between them.

3 Fill in the knotwork outlines with light blue, as marked on the chart.

4 Using dark blue, stitch in the outlines of the inner and outer borders as marked on the chart. Counting the stitches and squares carefully, stitch in the outlines of the birds, making sure that their beaks and stomachs are five squares apart.

5 Using red, yellow, green and purple, fill in the coloured areas of the birds and the straight borders as marked on the chart.

6 Using cream, fill in all the background areas behind the birds and the knots.

7 Sponge away any marks left from the water-soluble pen; when the embroidery is completely dry, press it gently from the back (see page 10). Pull the fabric back into square if it has distorted.

8 Trim the raw edges of the rug to within 1¹/2-2in (4-5cm) of the stitching. Cut the backing fabric to the same size; lay the backing fabric face up and cover it with the embroidery, face down. Pin and tack (baste) a seam just at the edge of the embroidery; stitch around this twice by machine, reinforcing the corners, and leaving about 20in (50cm) open for turning.

9 Clip the corners and trim the seams to about ³/4in (2cm), then turn the rug to the right side. Press under the seam allowances of the turning, and close it with slip stitch or ladder stitch. Press the rug gently from the back (see page 10).

PRACTICAL TIPS

Stitch the outlines of all the knotwork borders before you fill any of them in, and before you stitch the plain borders; it is much easier to see if you have miscounted before the light blue is added.

Keep checking your stitching to make sure that the birds align exactly.

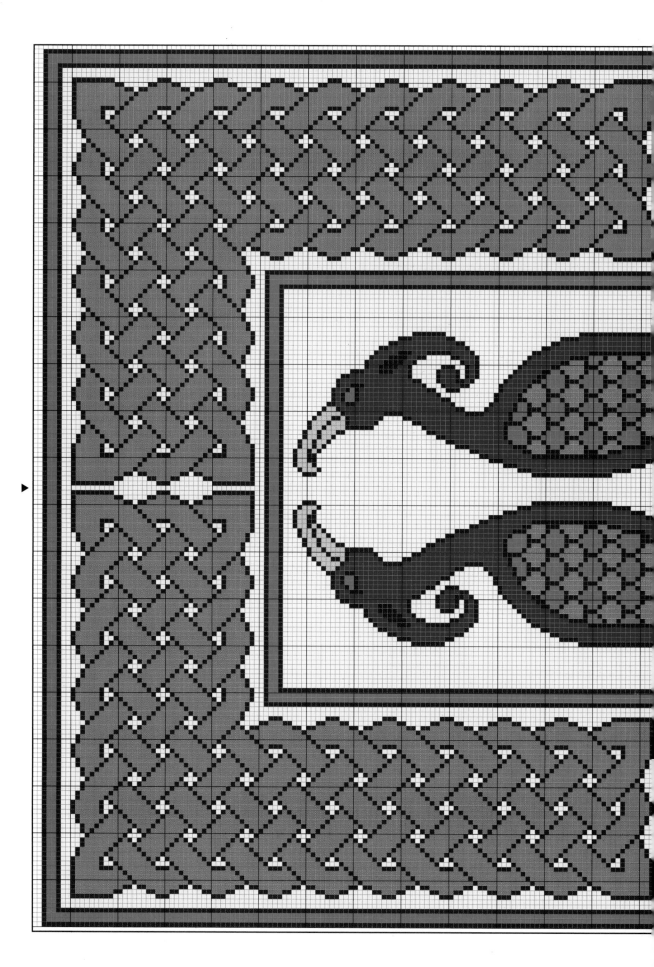

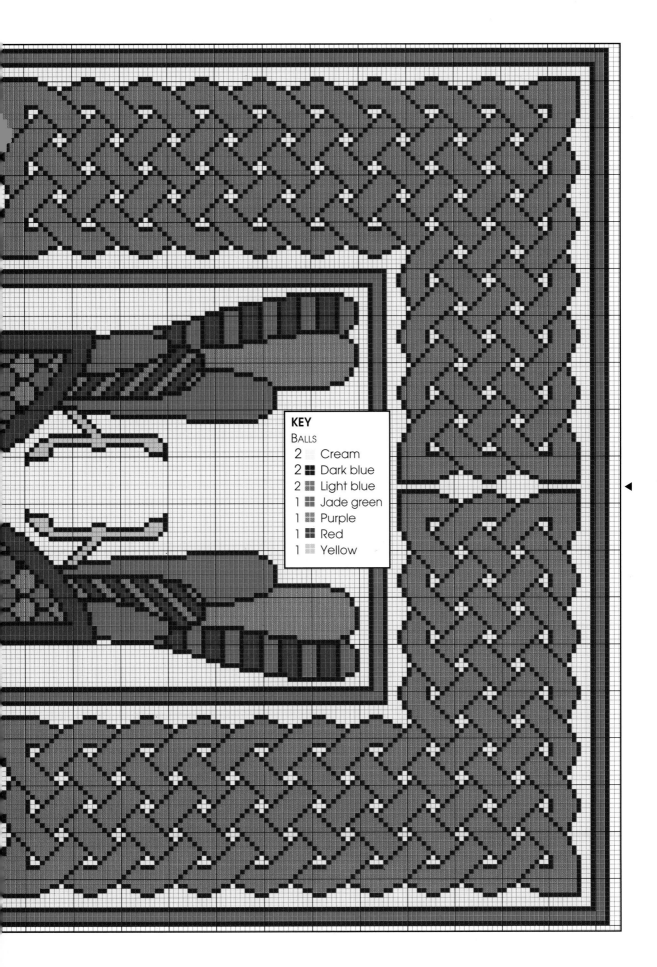

KEY
BALLS
2 ▢ Cream
2 ▦ Dark blue
2 ▦ Light blue
1 ▦ Jade green
1 ▦ Purple
1 ▦ Red
1 ▦ Yellow

CRATIO

7 uops fir godor

GUER

mid

ABUD

LETTERING

Celtic lettering is some of the most beautiful in history. In decorating their letterforms, Celtic scribes combined an exuberant use of colour with an aesthetic sensitivity that laid the foundations for the wonderful illuminated manuscripts of the Middle Ages.

There is no one style of Celtic lettering; even the great source-books, such as the *Book of Kells* and the *Book of Durrow* (written in Ireland in the eighth or early ninth centuries), contain several different styles within their pages. A typical illuminated page began with an elaborately decorated initial letter, sometimes made in the shape of a fantastic animal. Such letters were loosely based on the forms known as versals, but often they are so tortuous and interwoven that they are virtually unrecognisable as a letter; the 'S' on page 112 is based closely on one of these letters.

The illuminated letter might be followed by several lines of strange angular lettering, with or without extra angular knots within the shape, again often stylised beyond immediate recognition and with the spaces between them filled with flat, bright colours. The letters on page 86 and pages 80-85 reflect these particular styles.

Then the 'ordinary' text would begin, often some variation of the styles known as uncial and half-uncial – the letters on page 108 echo some uncial forms, and those on pages 72-77 are based on half-uncials from the *Book of Kells*. Occasionally throughout the text, at a break such as a new chapter, there might be a smaller, less elaborately decorated initial; the letters of the Noel decoration on page 90 and the animal letters on pages 100-107 reflect this simpler kind of illumination.

INITIAL CARDS

These wonderfully bright initials were taken from the *Book of Kells*; the monks working on that manuscript often filled in the counters (the spaces within letters) with areas of flat colour in mid-green, chalk-blue, mauve or pink, and then surrounded them with an outline of red brush dots or squares.

MATERIALS

For each large card you will need:
- One piece of cream Aida fabric, 11hpi, 8in (20cm) square
- One card blank with an aperture large enough to show your finished design
- Stranded cottons (floss) in the colours given in the key, plus one skein of your chosen filling colour
- Medium tapestry needle

For each small card you will need:
- One piece of cream Aida fabric, 14hpi, 8in (20cm) square
- One card blank with an aperture large enough to show your finished design
- Stranded cottons (floss) in the colours given in the key, plus one skein of your chosen filling colour

- One reel of fine red metallic embroidery thread, plus one reel of fine metallic thread to tone in with your chosen filling colour
- Fine tapestry needle

PRODUCING THE DESIGN

1 If you are working on 11hpi fabric, use three strands of cotton (floss) for your stitching. If you are working on 14hpi fabric, use two strands of cotton (floss). Begin with black, and stitch all of the main letter first.

2 If you are using 11hpi fabric, stitch the filling block or blocks in three strands of your chosen filling colour, and stitch the outline dots in three strands of red. If you are using 14hpi, use two strands of stranded cotton (floss) and one strand of the matching metallic thread for the filling block and the outline dots.

3 Press the design on the back using a steam iron (see page 10).

4 Follow the instructions on this page for making up the cards.

PRACTICAL TIP

Metal threads tend to shred quite easily so, to keep them in prime condition while you are stitching, only use short lengths.

MAKING UP CARDS

1 *Check that your design fits behind the aperture in the card front, then trim the fabric so that it fits inside the card with the design showing correctly at the front.*

2 *Lay the card blank face down on a flat surface and spread some paper glue around the edges of the aperture, making sure that glue does not go onto the front of the card. Use a medium amount of glue; if you use too much the card will buckle.*

3 *Carefully position the embroidered design so that it shows through the aperture. Smooth the edges of the fabric so that there are no wrinkles and so that they are caught by the glue.*

4 *With the card face down again, put a little glue around the edges of the left-hand flap. Don't put glue over the middle of this flap, otherwise it might come through the embroidery and spoil it. Fold the flap over the back of the embroidery and press into place.*

5 *Leave the card to dry, fully pressed between two heavy books.*

VARIATIONS

These initials would look pretty worked in paler colours as birth congratulation cards; stitch the main letter in a mid-pastel colour, then pick up toning pastels for the filling blocks and the dots round the outside.

Try stitching two initials on the same piece of background fabric for an unusual wedding or anniversary card. You could stitch the initials very small, perhaps using one strand of cotton on 18 or 22hpi fabric.

KEY
For both cards

DMC 310	Anchor 403	■	Black
DMC 326	Anchor 19	+	Red
Your chosen filling colour	/		

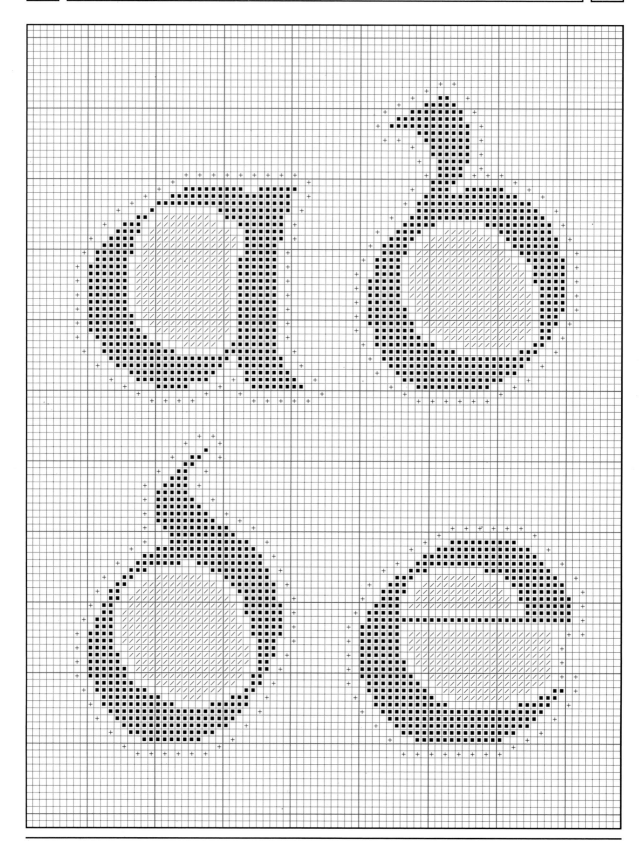

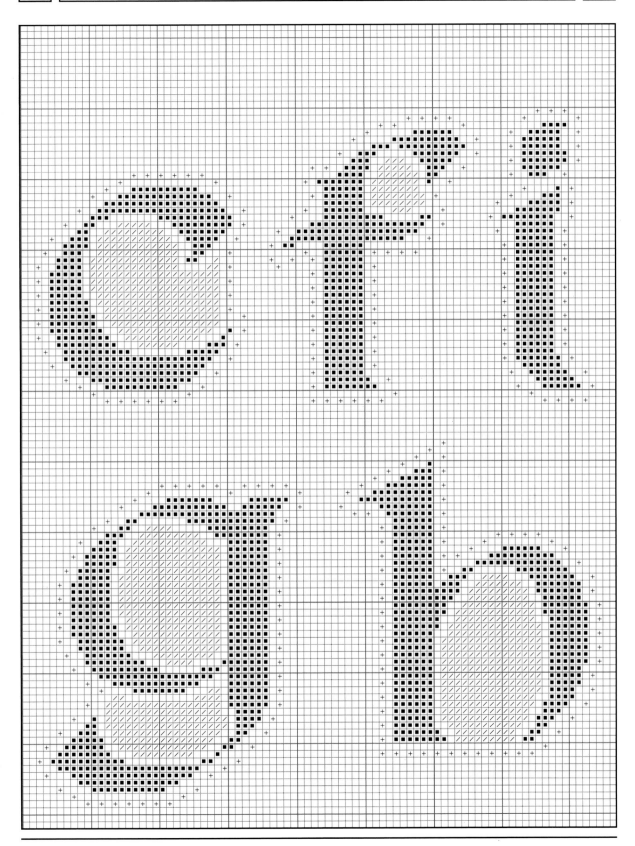

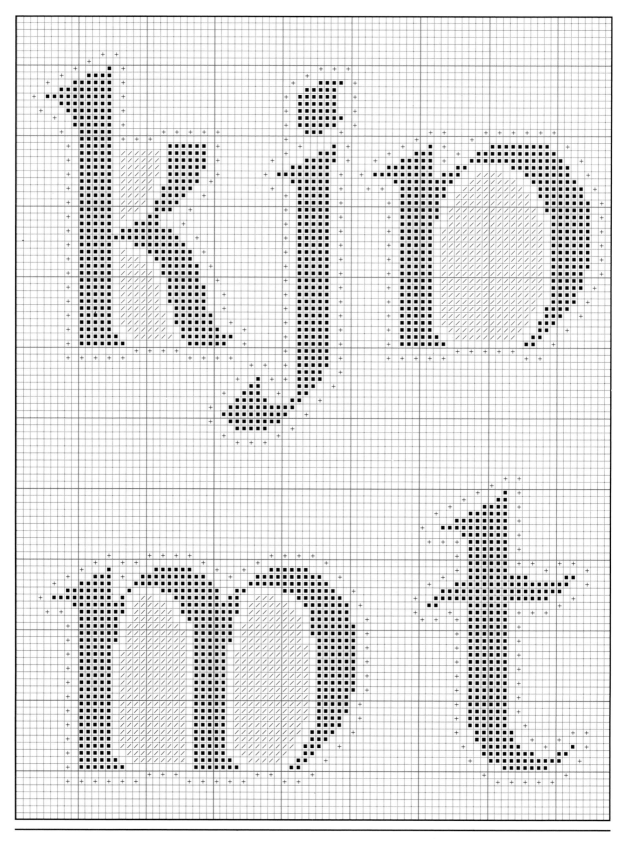

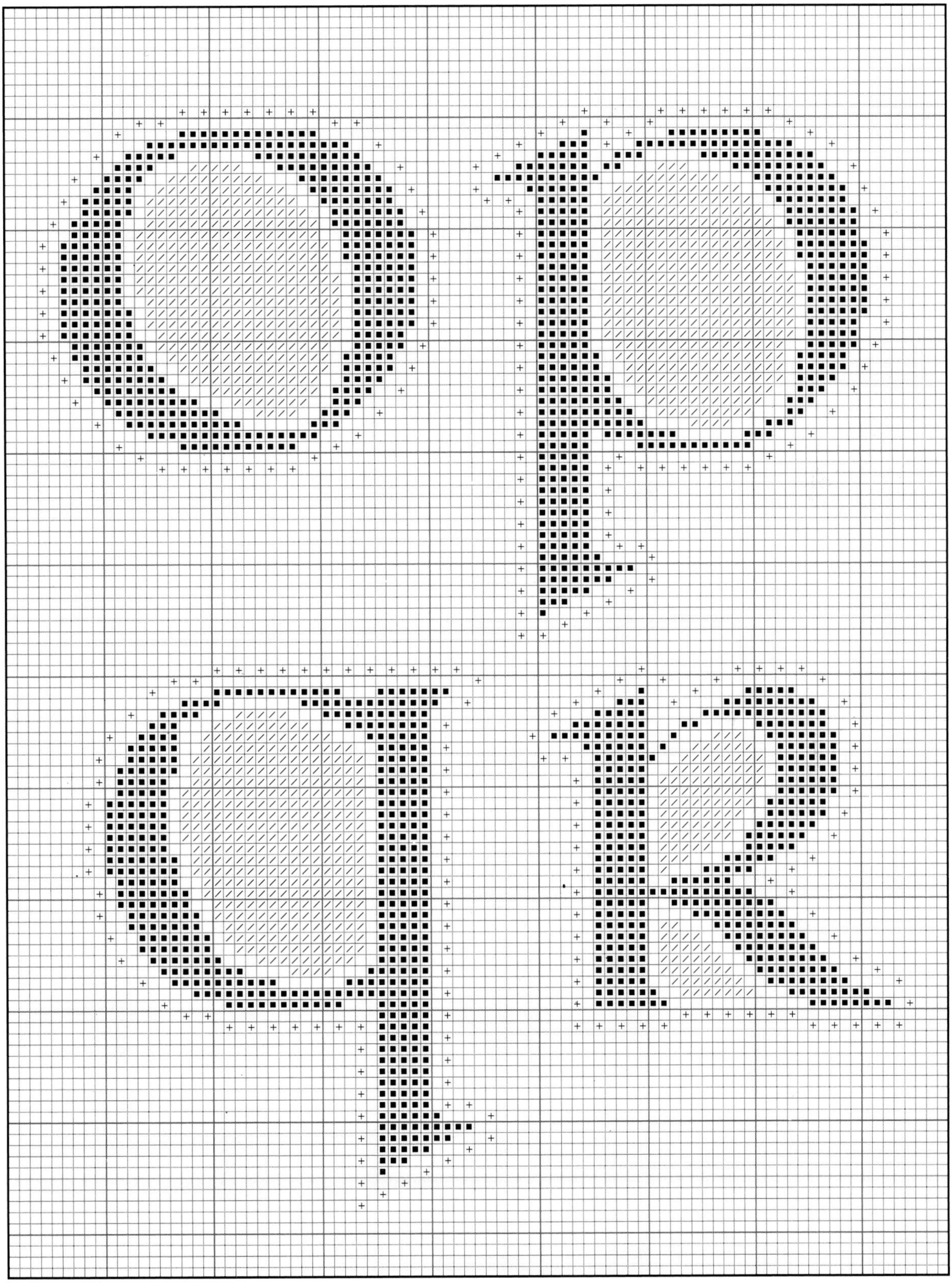

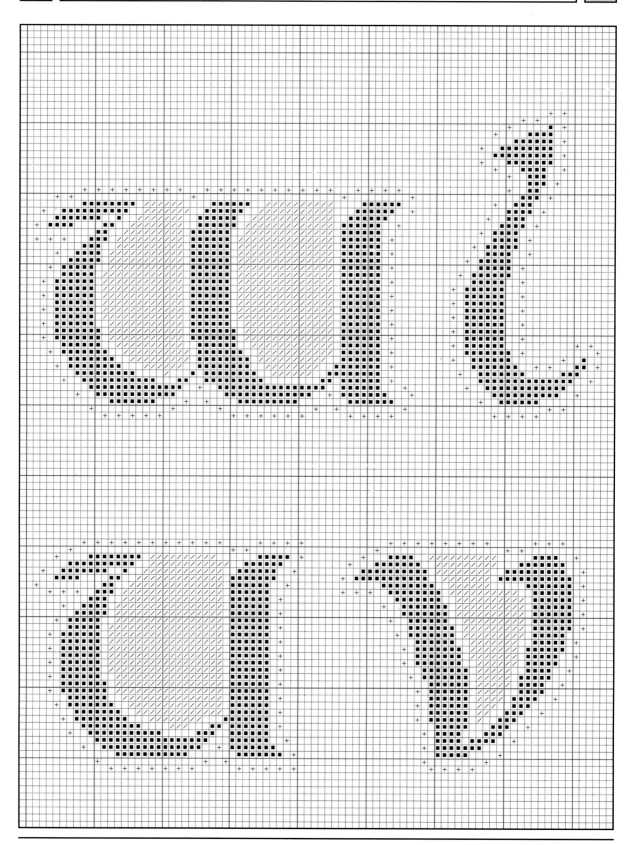

STITCHED NAMEPLATE

$\boxed{p}$ ersonalised presents are always well received. In this project one of the Celtic alphabets has been used to make a nameplate; you could adapt the same idea for a card or a sampler.

MATERIALS
- Graph paper or squared paper
- One strip of white Aida, 11hpi, 6in (15cm wide); for length, see instructions
- Stranded cottons (floss) in the colours given in the key
- Medium tapestry needle
- Mounting card in a matching colour, or frame to fit the finished embroidery

PRODUCING THE DESIGN

1 On the graph paper or squared paper, chart the name that you want to use on the nameplate using the letters from the sampler design on page 108. Space them so that they look correct visually; note that some of the letters go slightly above or below the standard level of the others.

2 Around your lettering, draw in the border design. There should be three clear squares between the edges of the lettering and the border at the sides, and between the standard letters (those that do not go above or below the level of the others) and the border at the top and bottom. Count or fold

your chart to find the centre line of the design.

3 Count the number of squares horizontally that your design now occupies; your strip of fabric will need to be that number of squares long, plus 1¹/4-1¹/2in (3-4cm) each end.

4 Fold the fabric strip in half to find the centre line and mark the line with tacking thread or a water-soluble pen. Measure down 3¹/2in (8.5cm) from the top of the strip and mark a horizontal line at this level; this line is the baseline guide for all the standard letters in your design.

5 Use three strands of cotton (floss) for all the cross stitches. Beginning at the centre of your chart and fabric, stitch the letters in light

green, aligning the bottoms of the standard letters with your baseline guide. Stitch the border, following the chart for the colours.

6 Using one strand of dark green, outline the letters in back stitch (see page 9). Using one strand of dark peach, outline the light peach border in back stitch as shown on the chart.

7 Remove the tacking threads, or sponge the embroidery to remove the pen marks and allow to dry completely. Press the embroidery from the back (see page 10).

8 Cut a mount from a matching piece of mounting card, or fit the the nameplate into a frame to complete it.

PRACTICAL TIP
It is important to space the letters by eye rather than by calculation when you are drawing up the chart; the different shapes of letters mean that some combinations seem closer together than others when they are positioned with the same gap between them.

KEY			
DMC 561	Anchor 210	+	Dark green
DMC 350	Anchor 11	■	Dark peach
DMC 352	Anchor 8	0	Light peach
DMC 350	Anchor 11	−	Dark peach
DMC 562	Anchor 208		Light green (for letters)

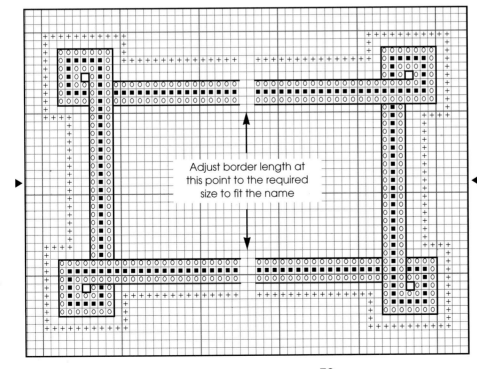

Adjust border length at this point to the required size to fit the name

VARIATIONS
Use this letterform to create a personalised card, taking just one initial and surrounding it with a shortened version of the border. Or put two names together and lengthen the sides of the border to take them both in.

PINCUSHION AND NEEDLECASE

K notted letterforms adorn this pincushion and needlecase set in toning colours. On the needlecase the initial is worked in peach on a white background; on the pincushion the pale peach letter on a darker background gives a more subtle effect.

MATERIALS
- One needlecase made for cross stitch in white Aida, 14hpi
- One piece of peach Aida, 14hpi, 6in (15cm) square
- Stranded cottons (floss) in the colours given in the key
- Fine tapestry needle
- Circular pincushion base with 4in (10cm) diameter cushion

PRODUCING THE DESIGN
1 Press the peach fabric and the needlecase. Fold the fabric in half lengthwise and press gently, and then fold in half across the width and press; make a dot in water-soluble pen where the folds cross to mark the centre of the fabric. Do the same with the needlecase front (ignore the fact that two of the corners are rounded).

2 Choose the initials that you want to use from the charts on the following pages. On each initial you choose, find the centre square and mark it with a pen dot; this will correspond to the dot you have marked on the fabric.

3 Using two strands of pale peach, follow the chart for your chosen letter to stitch the design onto the peach fabric for the pincushion. Using two strands of peach, stitch your chosen initial onto the front of the needlecase.

4 Using one strand of dark orange, work back

stitch (see page 9) around the edges of each letter and across the knotted part of each letter as marked on the charts.

5 Sponge away the marks made by the water-soluble pen, and when the embroideries are completely dry, press them from the back (see page 10).

6 Assemble the pincushion according to the manufacturer's instructions. This generally requires unscrewing the padded area from the base, stretching the embroidery over the pad (making sure that it is positioned in the centre), gluing or taping the fabric in place underneath the pad, and reassembling the pincushion.

PRACTICAL TIP
The centre-point of each letter is not always in the centre of the knot, so make sure that you measure and mark it correctly for each different initial that you work.

VARIATIONS
The whole alphabet is included in the charts, so you can personalise anything appropriate, or put several letters together to make a monogram.

Because these letters are so ornate, they tend not to work very well together for spelling out names, but they look effective worked into a sampler design.

KEY		
DMC 3341	Anchor 8	+ Peach *or*
DMC 3824	Anchor 6	+ Pale peach
DMC 606	Anchor 334	− Dark orange

BRIGHT SAMPLER

Τ he unusual design of this sampler is based on a style which Celtic scribes often used in illuminated manuscripts. The first row of words following an ornate capital letter would be written in straight-sided, sometimes bizarre, letterforms, with the gaps inside and between them (the counters) filled with bright colours.

Stitch count: 148 x 128
Design size: $11^1/2$ x $9^1/2$in (29 x 24cm)

MATERIALS
- One piece of white Aida, 14hpi, 16 x $13^1/2$in (40 x 34cm)
- Stranded cottons (floss) in the colours given in the key
- Fine tapestry needle
- Frame to fit the finished embroidery, with an aperture at least 13 x 11in (33 x 28cm)

The brightly-coloured counters within and between the letters are outlined with black back stitch

PRODUCING THE DESIGN
1 Press the fabric. Measure down $2^3/4$in (7cm) from the top of the fabric and 3in (7.5cm) in from the right-hand side; make a dot at the point in water-soluble pen. This is where you will begin stitching; it corresponds with the top right corner of the 'J' on the chart.
2 Using two strands of black, stitch the top row of letters, working from the 'J' across to the 'A'.
3 Count the squares and stitches carefully to see exactly where to begin the middle row of letters, then stitch them in the same way. Do the third row in the same way.
4 Using two strands of cotton (floss) in the appropriate colours for all the cross stitches, fill in the coloured areas of the design as marked on the chart.
5 Counting the squares and stitches carefully to check that the positioning is correct, stitch the black borders in cross stitch.
6 Using one strand of black, work back stitch (see page 9) around the edges of all the coloured panels.
7 Sponge away any marks left by the water-soluble pen; when the embroidery is completely dry, press it from the back (see page 10).
8 Assemble the embroidery in the frame, following the manufacturer's instructions.

PRACTICAL TIPS
If you are left-handed, or prefer to work from left to right, begin at the top left corner. In this case, measure $2^3/4$in (7cm) down and $3^1/2$in (8.5cm) in from the left; this spot corresponds to the top left of the bar at the top of the 'A'. Work the lettering before you stitch the border so that it will be easier to count the stitches of the border correctly.

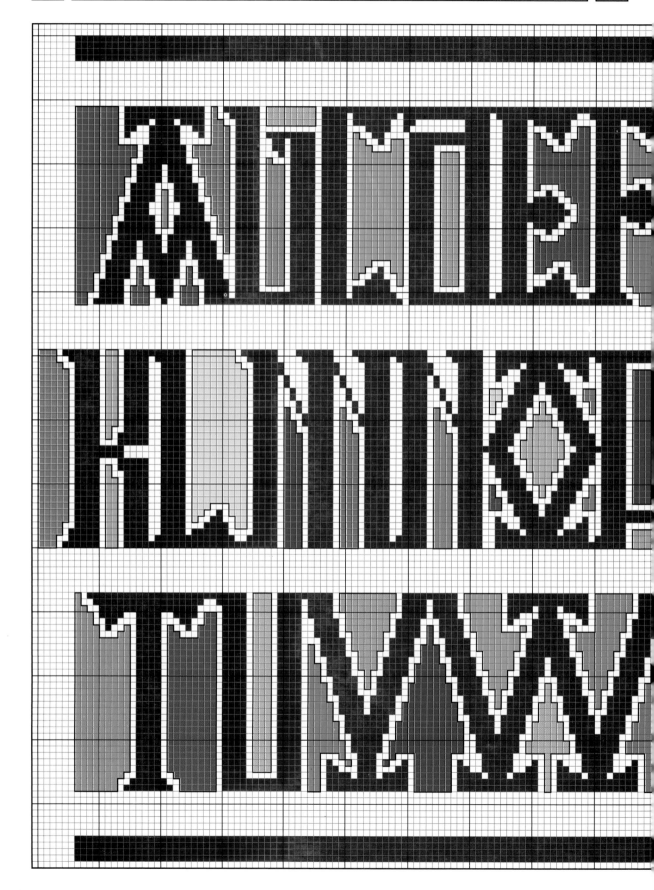

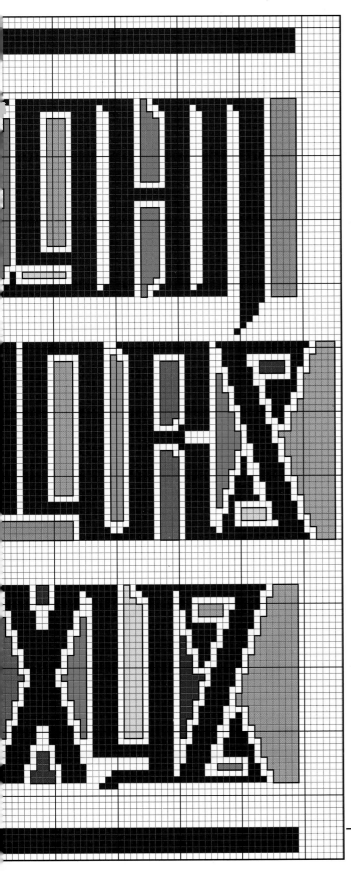

KEY

DMC 310	Anchor 403		Black (4 Skeins)
DMC 550	Anchor 102		Dark purple
DMC 333	Anchor 111		Light purple
DMC 820	Anchor 134		Royal blue
DMC 3812	Anchor 189		Jade green
DMC 742	Anchor 303		Yellow
DMC 740	Anchor 316		Orange
DMC 600	Anchor 63		Pink
DMC 995	Anchor 410		Turquoise
DMC 910	Anchor 228		Bright green
DMC 666	Anchor 9046		Red
DMC 310	Anchor 403	–	Black

VARIATION

This alphabet is composed of such strange letters that they do not work very well for making words; however, some of them look effective singly or in pairs as monograms.

NOEL CHRISTMAS DECORATION

Bright Christmassy colours are used in this richly illuminated Noel decoration; the glittering goldfingering and the sheen on the coton perlé provide extra opulence, and will catch the light from candles or Christmas tree lights.

Stitch count: 100 x 31
Design size: 10½ x 3½ (27 x 9cm)

MATERIALS

- One piece of plastic canvas, 12 x 4¾ in (30 x 12cm)
- Gauge 5 and gauge 3 coton perlé in the colours given in the key
- One reel of Twilley's dark or light gold goldfingering
- Large tapestry needle

PRODUCING THE DESIGN

1 Measure in ¾in (2cm) in from the right-hand side of the piece of plastic canvas (see page 9) and 2in (5cm) up. This is where you will begin stitching and corresponds to the top gold stitch on the right-hand edge of the tail of the 'L' on the chart.

2 Using one strand of goldfingering, stitch all the gold squares as marked on the chart.

3 Using one strand of red or green as appropriate, follow the chart to fill in all the complete and partial cross-shapes formed by the gold lattice.

4 Using one strand of gauge 5 blue, follow the chart to stitch the outlines of the letters.

5 Using small, sharp-pointed scissors, cut the shape out of the plastic canvas; make sure that you leave the edges intact of any holes that have stitching into them.

6 Using one strand of the gauge 3 thread, neaten the cut edges of the plastic shape by working a variation of cross stitch over the edges themselves; work a series of diagonal overcasting stitches in one direction, then cross them with stitches in the other direction. When you come to the top left of the 'N' and the top right of the 'L', make a buttonhole loop for hanging.

PRACTICAL TIP
When you are cutting the fiddly bits inside the letters, cut one hole at a time with the points of the scissors away from the embroidery.

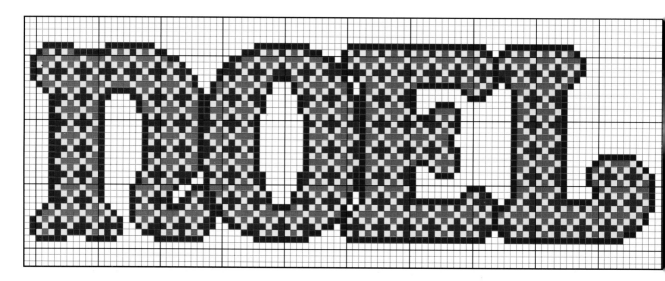

VARIATION

This design looks attractive worked on any scale; stitch it small on a long rectangle of even-weave fabric for a very special Christmas card.

KEY

Gauge 5:

DMC 498	Anchor 47	Red
DMC 820	Anchor 134	Blue
DMC 909	Anchor 923	Green
Goldfingering		Gold

Gauge 3:

DMC 796   Blue *(for edging)*

WEDDING INITIALS

S titch a pair of square initial pictures as a perfect wedding present. These chunky versal letterforms are each worked inside a square border, and embellished with pearl beads; the charts for each letter can be worked in blue or in pink.

Stitch count: 71 x 71
Design size: 6¼ x 6¼in (16 x 16cm)

MATERIALS

For each blue letter you will need:
• One piece of white Aida, 11hpi, 10in (25cm) square
• Stranded cottons (floss) in the colours given in the key
• Pack of small white pearl beads
• Medium tapestry needle
• White sewing thread

• Frame to fit the finished initial, with an aperture at least 7in (18cm) square

For each pink letter you will need:
• One piece of white Aida, 11hpi, 10in (25cm) square
• Stranded cottons (floss) in the colours given in the key
• Pack of small white pearl beads
• Medium tapestry needle
• White sewing thread
• Frame to fit the finished initial, with an aperture at least 7in (18cm) square

PRODUCING THE DESIGN

1 Press the fabric. Mark your starting point 2in (5cm) from the top and 2in (5cm) in from the right-hand side; make a dot with a water-soluble pen. The dot corresponds to the top right-hand stitch inside the border.

2 Using three strands of either dark blue or dark pink, depending upon your chosen colour scheme, follow the chart to work the alternating cross stitches that form the inner pattern of the border. Using three strands of light blue or light pink, work the light cross stitches as marked on the chart. Surround the pattern with the solid outlines of the border in one of the darker colours.

3 Measure or count to find the centre of the white square left inside the border; mark this with a dot of water-soluble pen. Choose the initial you want to use from the charts and mark the centre of it. Using three strands of the appropriate colours as marked on the chart and matching the centre of the chart with the central dot on your fabric, stitch the initial. Where a square is marked for a bead, leave it clear of stitching.

4 Sponge the fabric to remove any marks left by the water-soluble pen; when the fabric is completely dry, press it from the back (see page 10).

5 Using the white sewing thread, sew a pearl bead into each of the squares indicated on the charts for the letter and border.

6 Mount and frame the pictures together or separately.

KEY			SKEINS	
For each blue letter:				
DMC 798	Anchor 146	2	■	Dark blue
DMC 809	Anchor 140	2	+	Light blue
Bead			•	
For each pink letter:				
DMC 603	Anchor 68	2	■	Dark pink
DMC605	Anchor 60	2	+	Light pink
Bead			•	

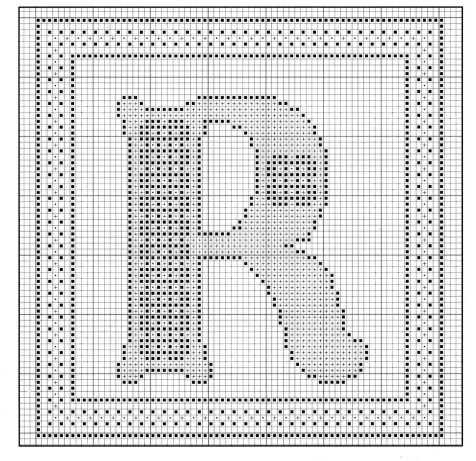

VARIATION
You don't have to use blue and pink for the initials; you can choose colours that match a particular room, or stitch the pictures in shades of yellow with gold or grey with silver for gold or silver wedding anniversaries.

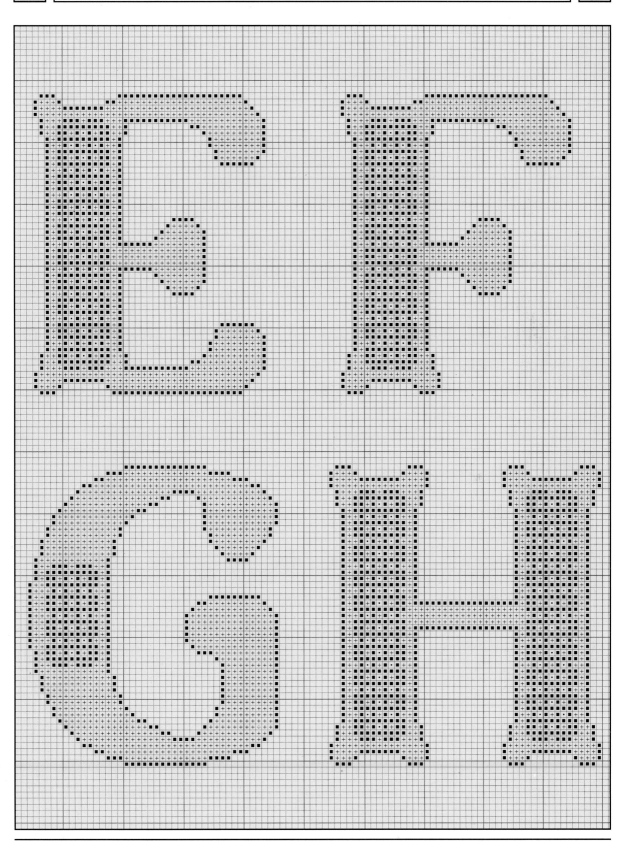

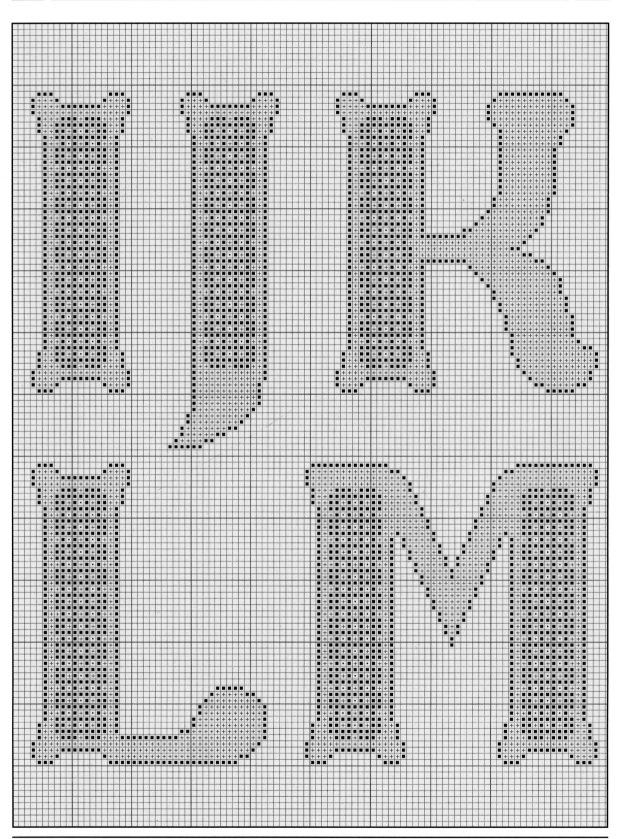

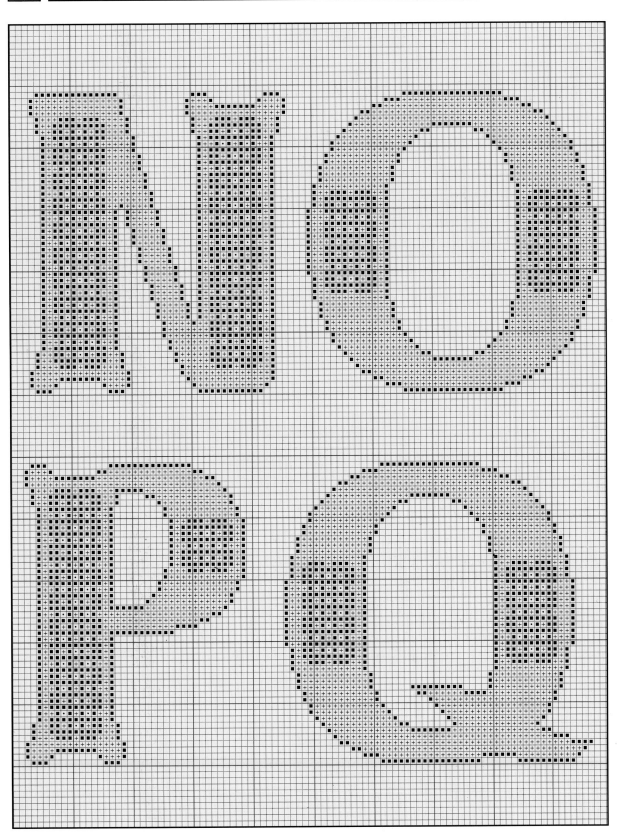

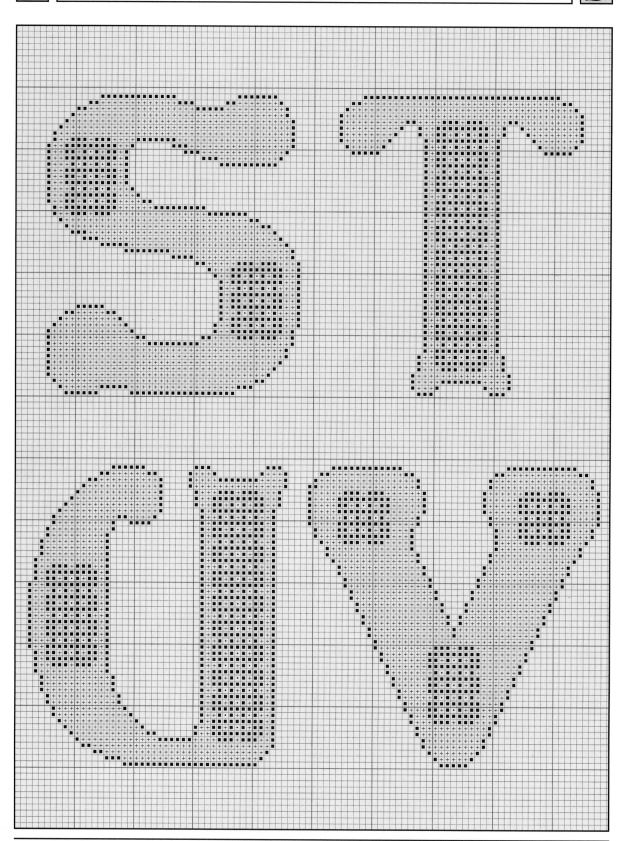

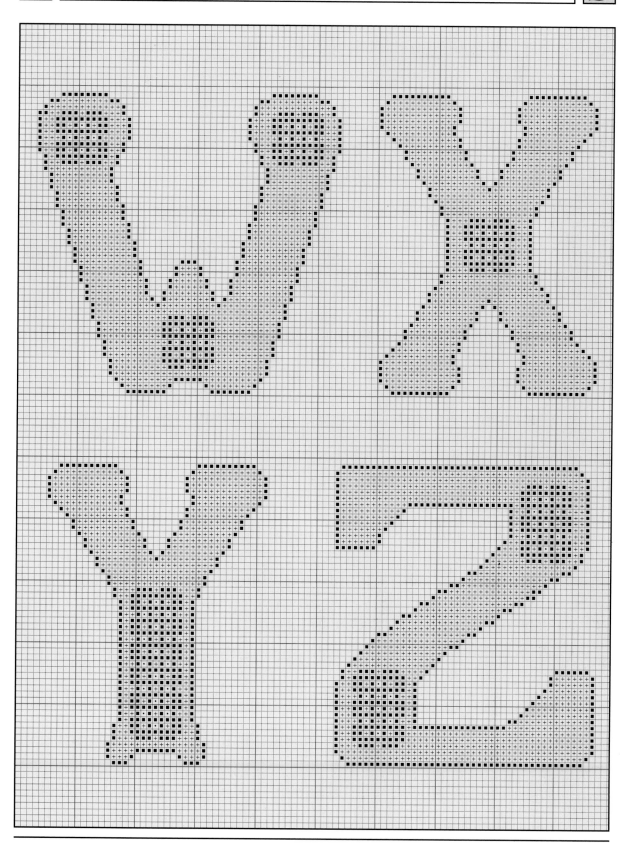

INITIAL PICTURES

Alphabets combining letterforms with strange animals appear frequently in Celtic art. The top finials of these letters are made from two birds' heads linked by a knot, with a simpler finial at the bottom.

MATERIALS

For each picture you will need:
- One damask embroidery square with a central panel at least 49 squares wide and 49 squares high
- Stranded cottons (floss) in the colours given in the key
- Fine tapestry needle
- Frame to fit the finished picture

PRODUCING THE DESIGN

1 Press the fabric. Count the squares of the central embroidery panel and mark the

centre-point with a dot of water-soluble pen.
Count and mark the centre of your chosen
initial on the chart.

2 Using two strands of embroidery cotton
(floss) in the appropriate colours, follow the
chart to stitch the initial on the damask
square.

3 Using one strand of dark blue, work back
stitch (see page 9) around the edge of the
initial as well as on the finials as indicated
on the chart.

4 Sponge the fabric to remove any marks from
the water-soluble pen; when it is completely
dry, iron it from the back (see page 10).

5 Assemble the picture in the frame, following
the manufacturer's instructions.

PRACTICAL TIP
*These initials use only a small amount of
thread; even if you are stitching several letters,
you will still only need one skein of each colour
of stranded cotton (floss).*

VARIATIONS
*These initials have been worked as small
pictures on damask squares, but they can be
worked just as easily on any counted thread
fabric.*

*If you want to use them as monograms on
non-even-weave fabric, such as a bag or a
dressing-gown, use the waste canvas method
(see page 10).*

KEY

DMC 986	Anchor 211	•	Dark green
DMC 989	Anchor 243	0	Light green
DMC 891	Anchor 29	+	Dark pink
DMC 893	Anchor 27	\	Light pink
DMC 796	Anchor 178	■	Dark blue
DMC 796	Anchor 178	-	Dark blue

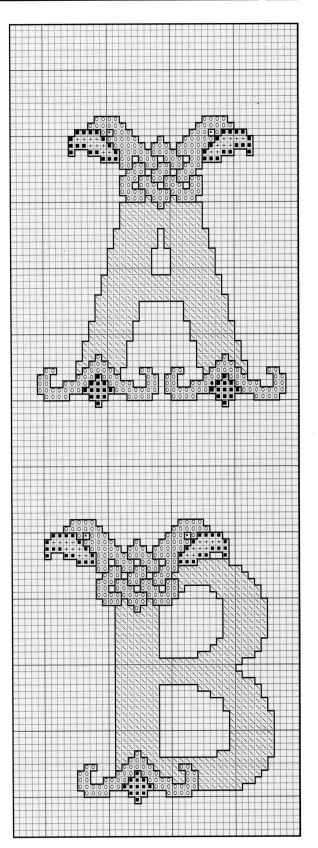

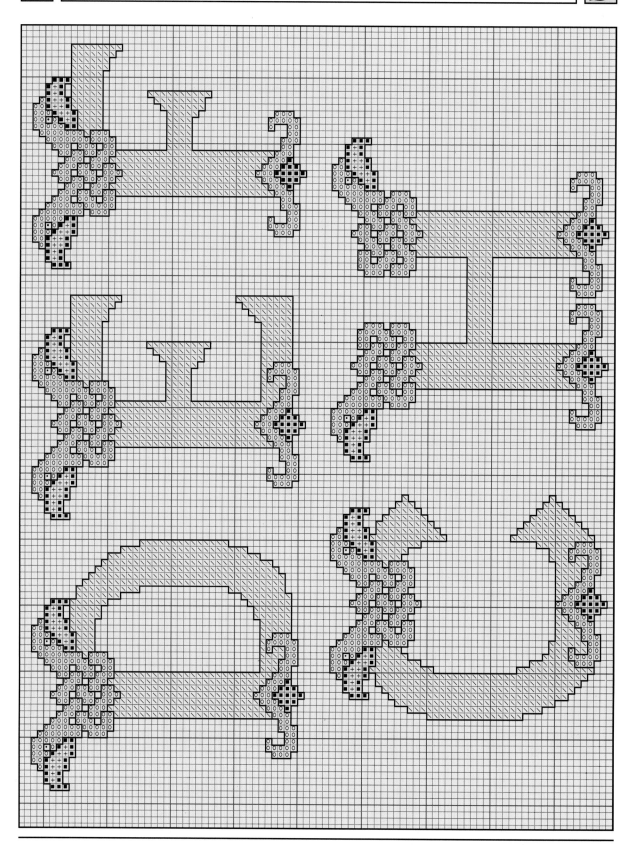

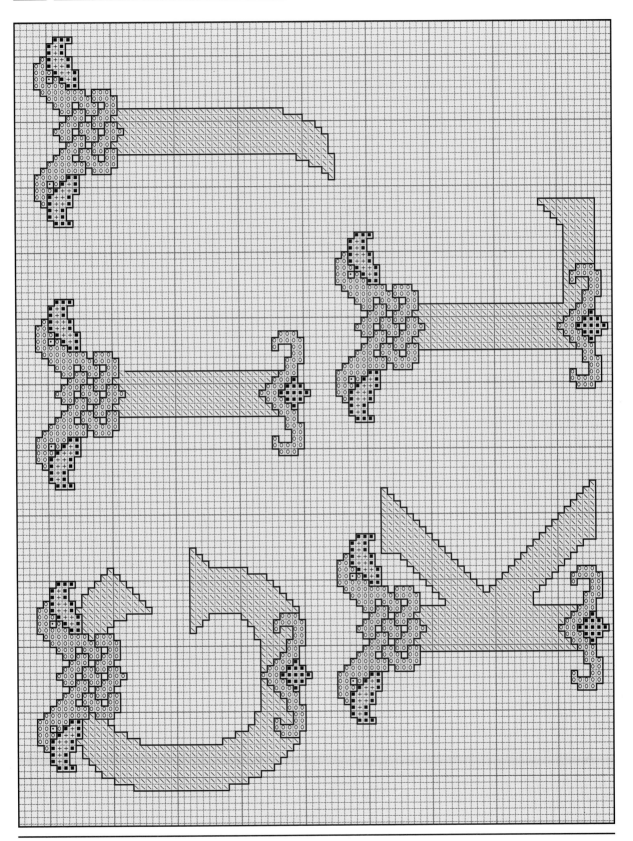

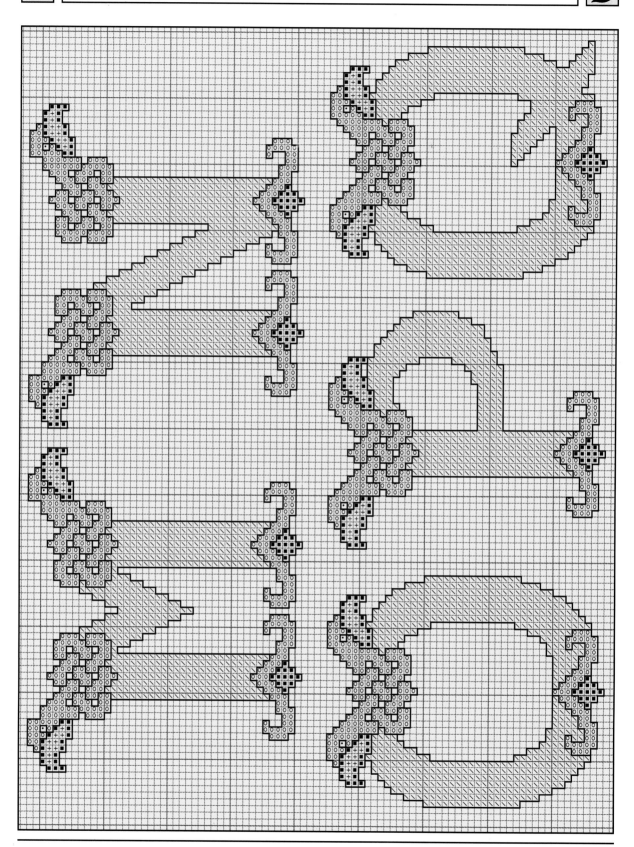

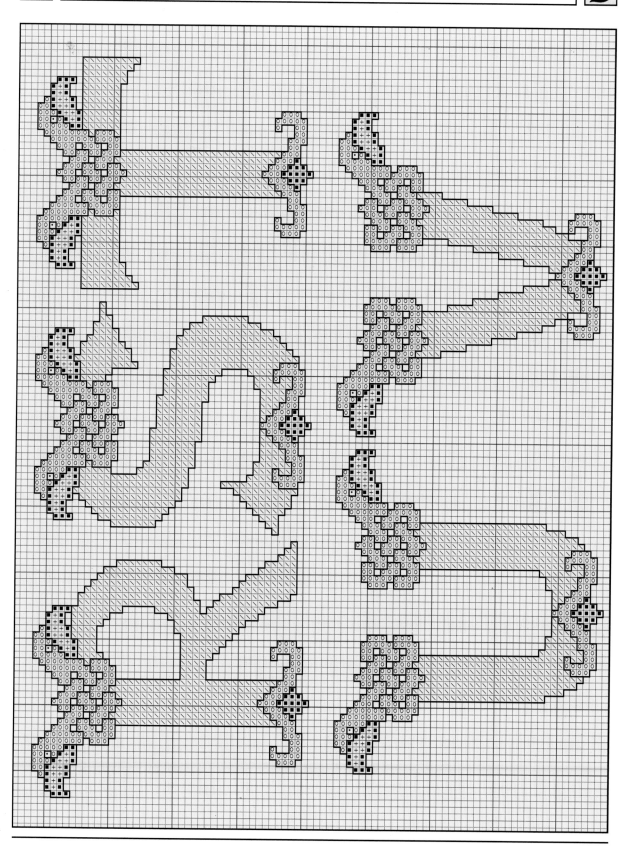

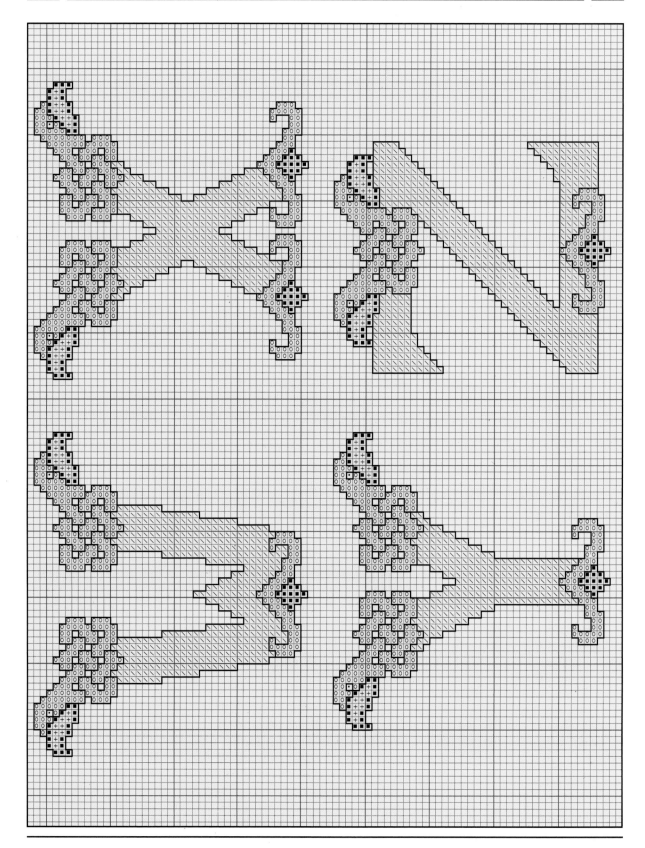

ᏆᎥᎬ ᎪᏁᗪ ᎻᎪᏁᗪᏦᎬᏒᏟᎻᏆᎬᏚ

A plain tie and handkerchief can be
personalised for a special man,
using Celtic letters and motifs. The tie is
embroidered with a monogram, while
the handkerchief sports the birds' head
finial from the decorated initials on
pages 101-106.

MATERIALS
- Small amount of waste canvas, 11hpi
- One plain blue tie
- One plain white man's handkerchief
- Anchor Marlitt thread in the colours given in
  the key
- Medium crewel needle

PRODUCING THE DESIGN
1 Select the initial you want to use from the
  charts on pages 101-106, then cut a piece of
  waste canvas covering the required number
  of squares. Tack the waste canvas (*see* page
  10) in position on the front of the fabric;

using two strands of silver-grey Marlitt, stitch
the initial over the waste canvas.

2 Cut a piece of waste canvas 3½ x 1½in
  (8.5 x 4cm); tack it to one corner of the
  handkerchief so that its central line is at 45°
  to each side of the fabric and the bottom is
  about 3½in (8.5cm) in from the corner.

3 Follow any of the charts showing the double
  birds' head, using two strands of silver-grey
  for the main part, blue for the beak outline,
  purple for the beak, and red for the eye. Use
  one strand of dark grey for the back stitch
  (*see* page 9).

4 Follow the instructions on page 10 for
  removing the waste canvas.

KEY (Marlitt)		
Anchor 845	O	Silver-grey
Anchor 836	■	Blue
Anchor 817	+	Purple
Anchor 815	•	Red
Anchor 846	–	Dark grey

VERSAL SAMPLER

The letterforms in this sampler are based on the forms known as missal versals; these shapes were used for the decorative initials in many illuminated manuscripts. The colour-scheme of yellow, green and purple picks up one of the more unusual colourways used by Celtic artists.

Stitch count: 141 x 165
Design size: 12 x 10in (30 x 26cm)

MATERIALS

- One piece of pale yellow Aida, 14hpi, 14 x 16in (35 x 40cm)
- Stranded cottons (floss) in the colours given in the key
- Fine tapestry needle
- Frame to fit the finished embroidery, with an aperture at least 12 x 10½in (30 x 27cm)

This detail shows the attractive shapes of some of the letterforms

PRODUCING THE DESIGN

1 Press the fabric, then fold it in half to give a line down the centre; mark the line with a water-soluble pen. Measure 2¾in (7cm) down this line from the top of the fabric and make a dot with the water-soluble pen. This corresponds with the central stitch of the upper line of the cross at the top of the chart.
2 Using two strands of dark purple, stitch the outline cross shape; then stitch the inner sections in light purple and dark purple as shown on the chart.
3 Using two strands of dark green, stitch the outline squares to the right and left of the cross; using light green, stitch the patterns inside them.
4 Continue working around the frame of the sampler in the same way, following the colours and patterns marked on the chart.
5 Counting the stitches and squares carefully, stitch the letters inside the border using two strands of light green.
6 Sponge away the marks made by the water-soluble pen, and when the embroidery is completely dry, press it from the back (see page 10).
7 Assemble the embroidery in the frame, following the manufacturer's instructions.

PRACTICAL TIPS

It might be tempting to stitch all the outlines of the border blocks first, but if you fill them in with the appropriate patterns as you go, you will be able to see more quickly if you have miscounted anywhere.
When you come to stitch the letters, you may find it easier to begin at the centre line of each row of letters and work outwards to the sides.

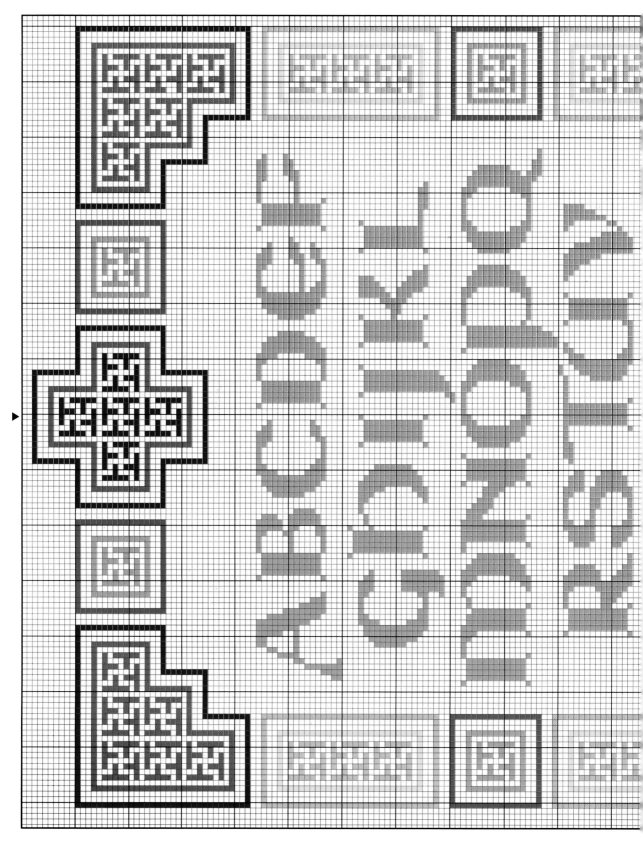

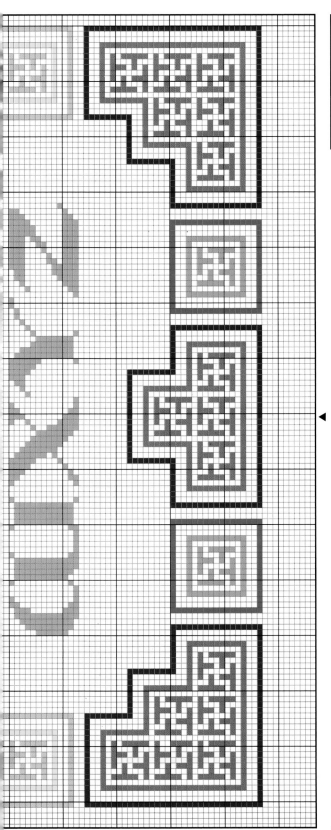

KEY

DMC 333	Anchor 101	▩	Dark purple
DMC 340	Anchor 98	▩	Light purple
DMC 912	Anchor 243	▩	Dark green
DMC 954	Anchor 240	▩	Light green (2 Skeins)
DMC 743	Anchor 302	▩	Dark yellow
DMC 744	Anchor 301	▩	Light yellow

ILLUMINATED INITIAL

T his opulently illuminated letter 'S' makes a wonderful picture; the gold outlines show off the bright colours of the solid sections and the cream backing fabric imitates the colour of vellum or parchment. The design is based on an initial taken from a French psalter.

Stitch count: 114 x 139
Design size: 10 x 12in (26 x 30cm)

MATERIALS

- One piece of cream Aida, 11hpi, 16 x 18in (40 x 45cm)
- Three spools of gold thread, Gütermann metallic 24
- Stranded cottons (floss) in the colours given in the key
- Medium tapestry needle
- Frame to fit the finished embroidery, with an aperture at least 11 x 14in (28 x 35cm)

The coloured areas of the design are set off by gold outlines

PRODUCING THE DESIGN

1 Press the fabric. Measure in $2^3/4$in (7cm) from the right-hand side of the fabric and $2^3/4$in (7cm) down from the top and mark the point with a dot of water-soluble pen. This dot marks the point at which you will begin stitching and corresponds to the top right corner of the frame on the chart. Using three strands of gold thread, and beginning at the marked dot, stitch all the gold outlines and diagonal lines of the frame.

2 Using three strands of stranded cotton (floss), fill in the red and blue stripes of the frame as appropriate.

3 Using three strands of gold thread, stitch all the gold outlines and dots of the 'S' design. Using three strands of stranded cotton (floss) in the appropriate colours, fill in all the solid areas as marked on the chart.

4 Sponge away the dot made by the water-soluble pen; when the embroidery is completely dry, iron it from the reverse (see page 10).

5 Assemble the embroidery in the frame, following the manufacturer's instructions.

PRACTICAL TIPS
Because there are strong diagonal lines in this design, you may find that the fabric has pulled out of square when you have finished the embroidery. If so, dampen it with a water spray, then pin it out square, using rust-resistant pins, on a pinboard protected by clean paper. When it is dry, iron it with a little spray-on starch to keep it square.
If you are left-handed, or prefer to stitch from left to right, begin your stitching at the top left corner of the frame; in this case, measure in from the top and the left-hand side of the fabric.

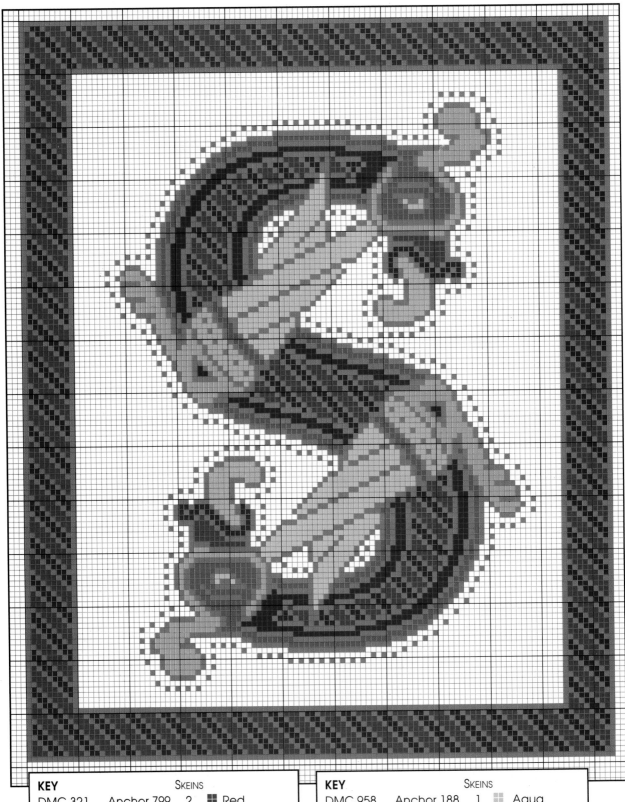

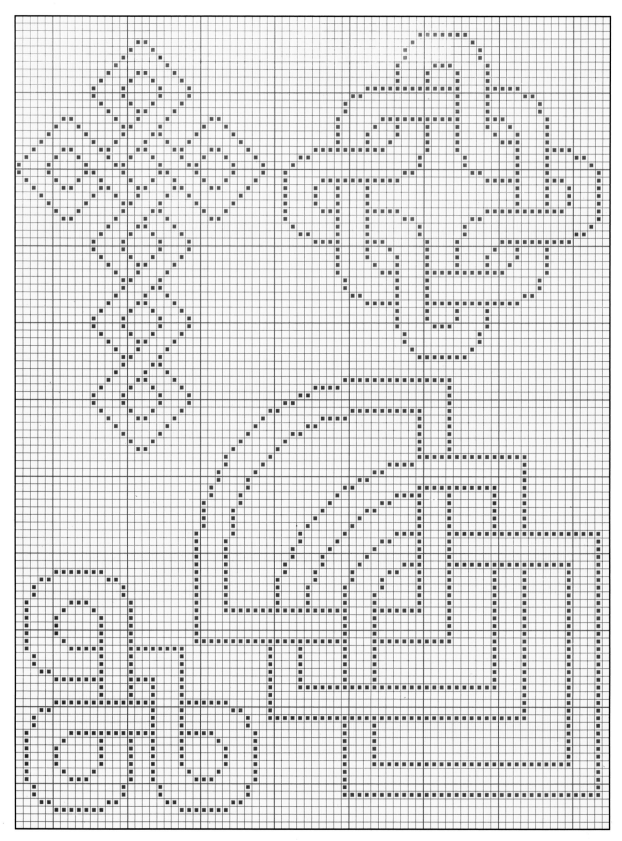

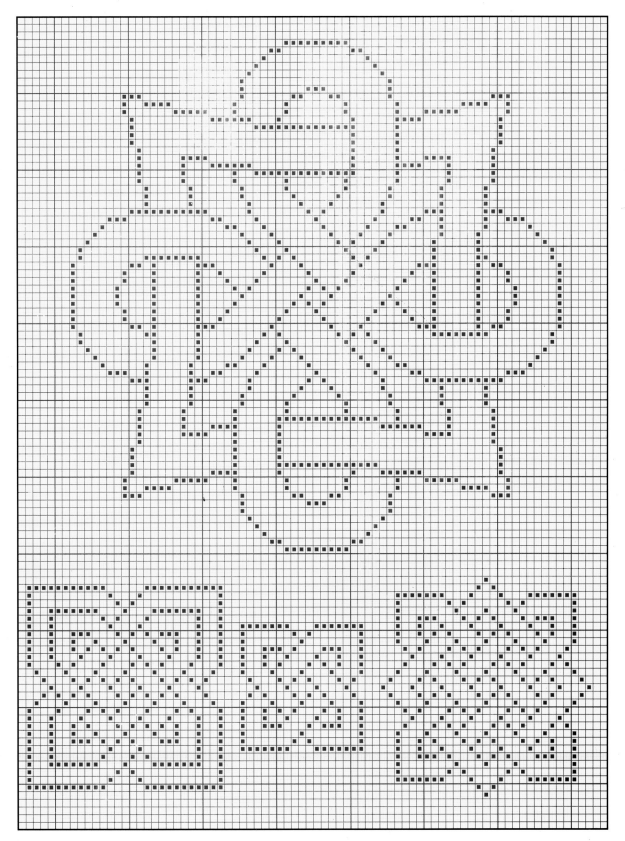

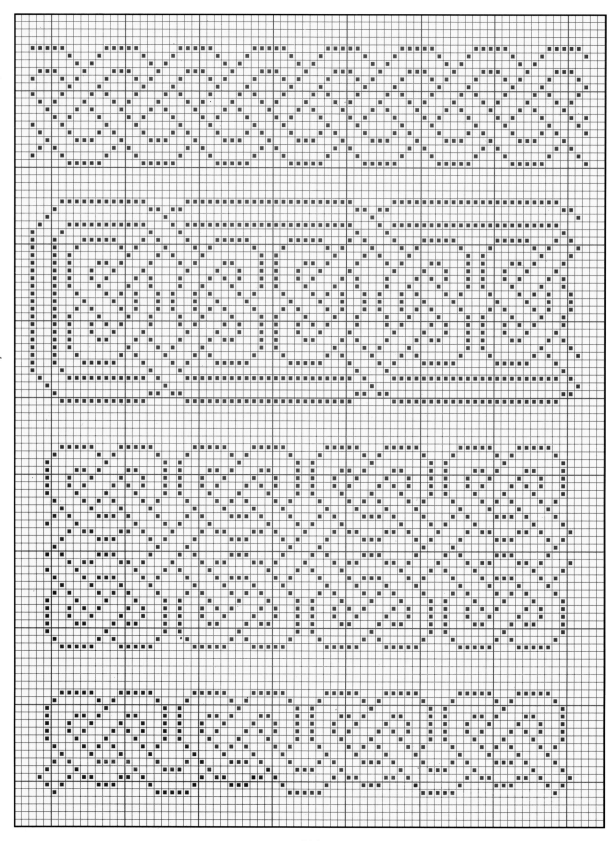

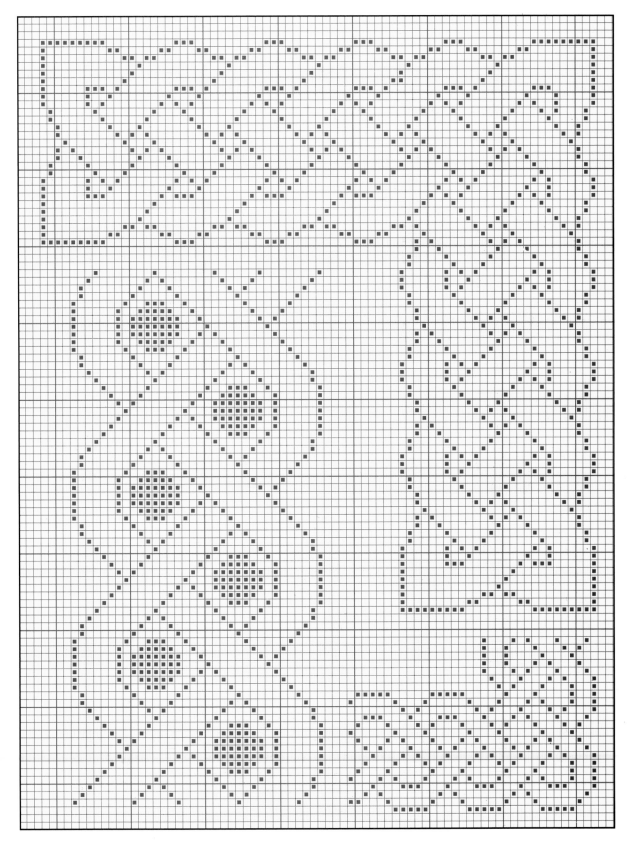

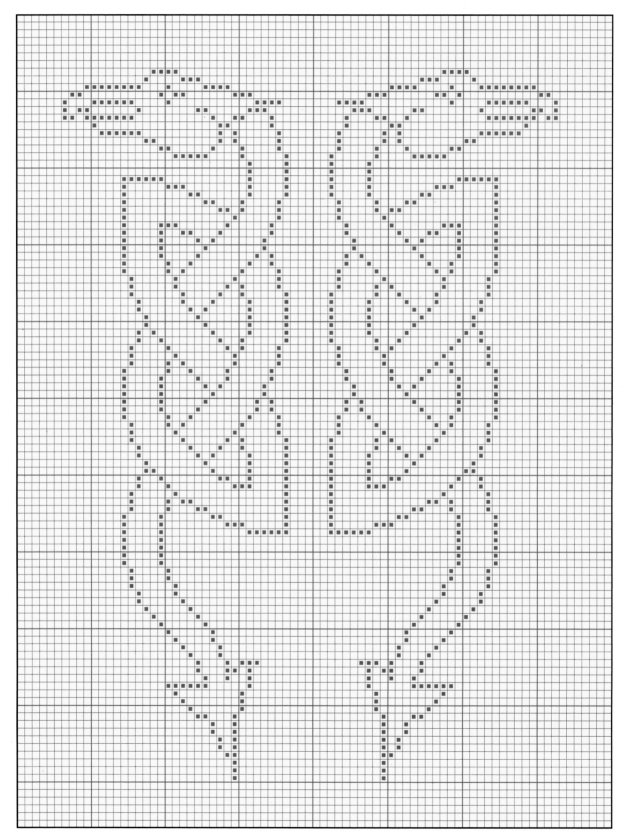

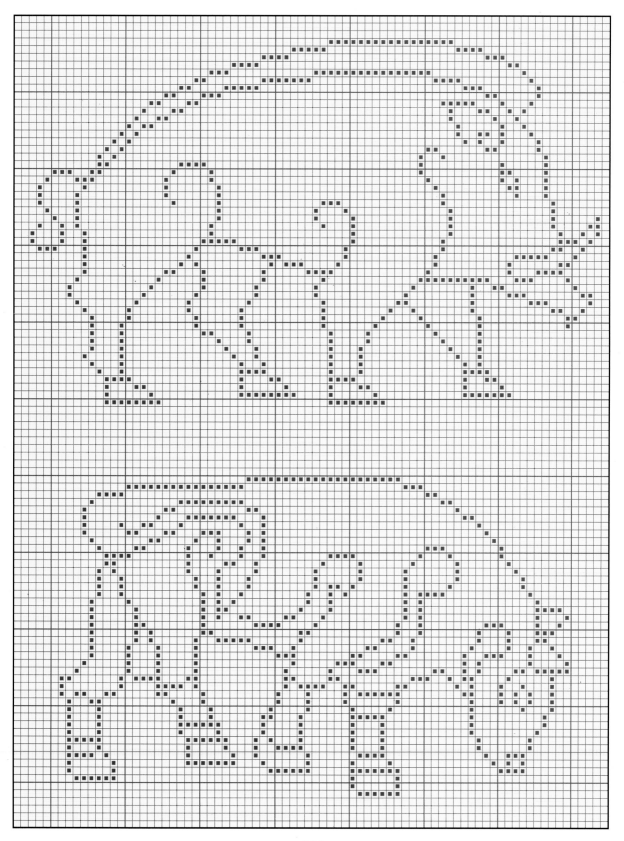

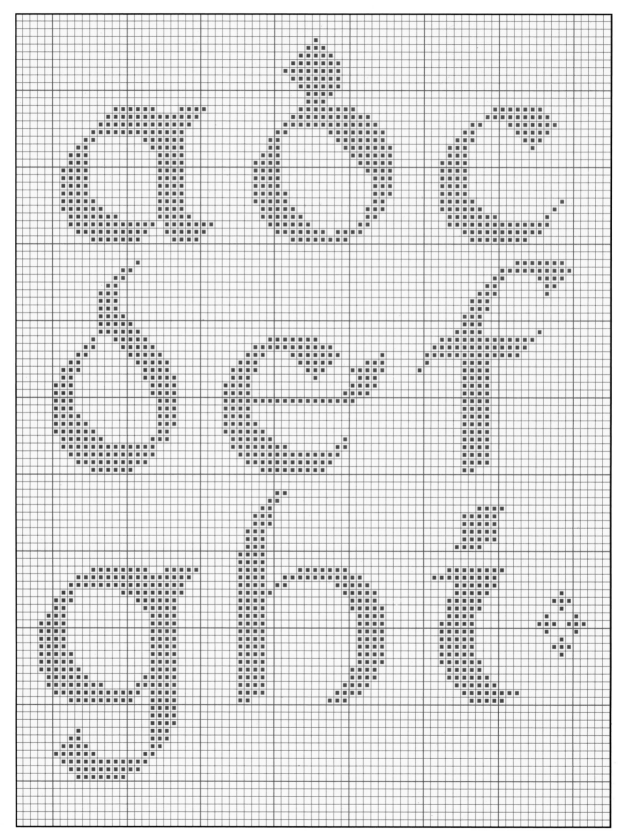

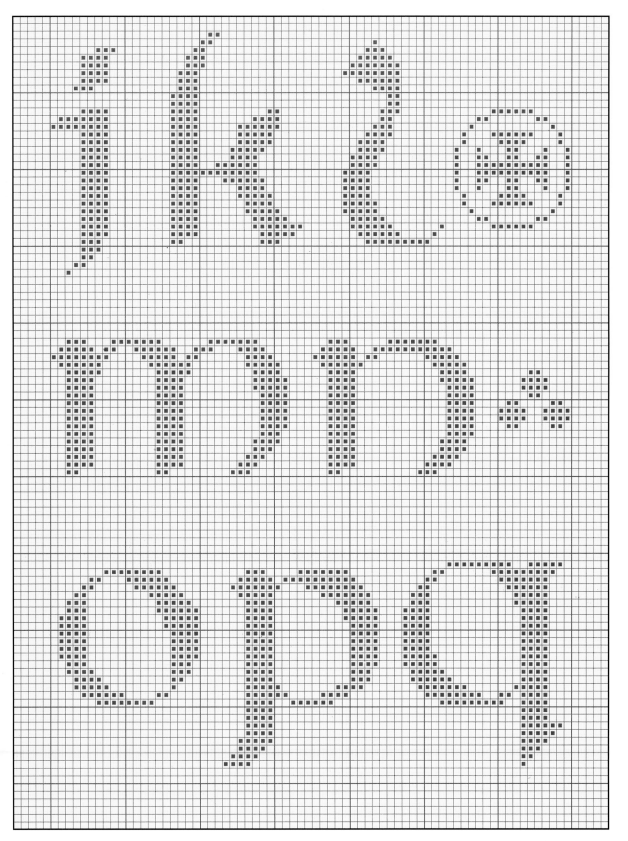

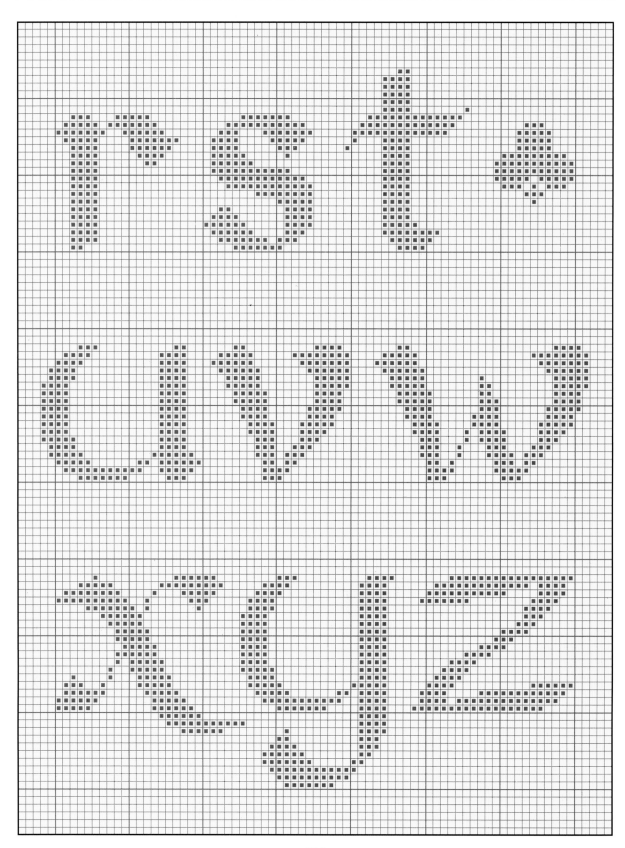

ACKNOWLEDGMENTS

All designs are by Gail Lawther. Many thanks to the following embroiderers for stitching some of the designs:
Beryl Hoad: *knotwork cushion, serpent pincushion.* Sarah Hoad: *horse picture, lion picture, stitched nameplate.* Liz Lance: *tablemats and napkins, initial pictures.* Christopher Lawther: *Celtic rug.* Doreen Newnham: *trinket box, wedding initials.* Pauline Oakes: *stained-glass angel, pincushion and needlecase.* Jennie Ring: *curtain tie-back.* Sue Slide: *initial cards, knotwork cards, knotwork picture, illuminated initial.*

Photograph credits:
The illustrations on the section opener pages are all taken from the late seventh century manuscript book *The Lindisfarne Gospels* and used by permission of The British Library.
pages 12-13 Cotton Ms Nero D. iv G 138b
pages 36-37 Cotton Ms Nero D. iv G 210b
pages 2, 68-69 Cotton Ms Nero D. iv G 211

SUPPLIERS
Items for cross stitch can be bought in many craft shops and from many mail-order craft companies. Suppliers of particular specialist items include:
Trinket boxes and jewellery blanks:
Martin Laundon, MP Products, 33 Whitefield Road, New Duston, Northampton NN5 6SJ
Framecraft Miniatures Ltd, 372-376 Summer Lane, Hockley, Birmingham B19 3QA
Specialist frames:
S & A Frames, 12 Humber Street, Cleethorpes, South Humberside DN35 8NN
Damask cross-stitch panels:
Crafty Ideas, The Willows, Cassington Road, Eynsham, Witney, Oxon OX8 1LF
Perforated jewellery blanks:
Needle Needs, Unit 21A Silicon Centre, 26-28 Wadsworth Road, Perivale, Middx UD6 7JD
General needlecraft and cross stitch supplies:
Pick n' Choose The Craft People, 56 Station Road, Northwich, Cheshire CW9 5RB

BIBLIOGRAPHY

If you would like to design your own Celtic cross stitch patterns, or to know more about Celtic art, the following books are recommended:
Celtic Design: Knotwork
Celtic Design: Illuminated Letters
Celtic Design: a Beginner's Manual
All by Aidan Meehan, published by Thames & Hudson, 1992
Celtic Stencil Designs by Co Spinhoven, published by Dover, 1990

Decorative Celtic Alphabets by Mallory Pearce, published by Dover, 1992
Celtic Art: the Methods of Construction by George Bain, published by Constable, 1992
Celtic Knotwork by Iain Bain, published by Constable, 1992
Celtic and Anglo-Saxon Painting by Carl Nordenfalk, published by Chatto & Windus, 1977

INDEX

Aida, 9; tape, 21
Angels, 7, 37, 51
Animals, 7, 14, 37, 38, 46, 48, 69, 100, 122-3

Baby's bib, 40
Backstitch, how to work, 9; on charts, 11
Binca, 9
Birds, 7, 14, 37, 40, 42, 54, 64, 100
Book of Durrow, 69
Book of Kells, 7, 69, 70
Bookmark, 14

Canvas, 9
Carpet pages, 13, 60
Celtic, art, 7, 13, 37, 69; patterns, 7, 8, 13; peoples, 7
Christening robe, 30
Christmas decoration, 90
Cockerel sweatshirt, 54
Colour schemes, 7, 13, 60, 109
Coton à broder, 10
Coton perlé, 10
Cross patterns, 14, 60, 116
Cross stitch, charts 10, 11; paper, 9; tips, 8-9; ways of working, 8-9
Curtain tie-back, 56
Cushion, 32

Design size, 11
Dolls' house rug, 22
Durrow, Book of, 69

Even-weave fabric, 9

Fabric gauge, 11
Fading pen, 10
Fish, 37, 56
Floss, 10

Frames, embroidery, 10-11

Greetings cards, 18, 38, 70

Half-uncial letterforms, 69
Handkerchief, 107
Hand towel, 20
Horse card and picture, 38
Horseman picture, 60

Illuminated initial, 112
Illumination, 7, 13, 26, 51, 69, 86, 109, 112
Initial, cards, 70; illuminated, 112; pictures, 100; wedding, 92
Ireland, Celtic tradition in, 7, 69

Jewellery, 26

Kells, Book of, 7, 69, 70
Key and fret patterns, 7, 13, 120-1
Knitting yarns, 10, 64
Knotwork patterns, 7, 8, 13-35, 64, 100, 115-19

Letterforms, 7, 69, 70-114, 124-6
Linen, 9
Lion picture, 46

Making up cards, 71
Marking pens, 10
Marlitt, 10
Metallic threads, 10

Nameplate, 78
Needlecase, 80
Needles, 9, 10
Noel Christmas decoration, 90

Peacock waistcoat, 42

People, 7, 37, 51, 60
Petit point 22, 38
Picture, angel, 51; horse, 38; horseman, 60; initial, 100; knotwork, 28; lion, 46; wedding initials, 92
Pincushion, knotted, 80; serpent, 48
Plastic canvas, 9
Pressing embroidery, 11

Rug, Celtic, 64; dolls' house, 22

Samplers, bright, 86; versal, 109
Serpent pincushion, 48
Sewing equipment, 10
Silk gauze, 9
Soft cotton, 10
Spiral patterns, 13,14, 26, 120
Stained-glass angel, 51
Stitch count, 11
Stranded cotton (floss), 10
Sutton Hoo jewellery, 7
Sweatshirt, cockerel, 54

Table mats and napkins, 24
Tapestry, needles, 9,10; yarn, 10
Threads, adjusting for different designs, 11; types of, 10; untwisting, 9
Tie and handkerchief, 107
Trinket box, 16

Uncial letterforms, 69

Versal letterforms, 69, 109

Waistcoat, peacock, 42
Waste canvas, 10, 25, 29, 30, 54
Water-soluble pen, 10, 11
Wedding initials, 92